Martin Luther King and the Civil Rights Movement

John A. Kirk

PEARSON

Harlow, England • London • New York • Boston • San Francisco • Toronto • Sydney
Auckland • Singapore • Hong Kor   hi
Cape Town • São Paulo • M

PEARSON EDUCATION LIMITED

Edinburgh Gate
Harlow CM20 2JE
United Kingdom
Tel: +44 (0)1279 623623
Web: www.pearson.com/uk

First published 2013 (print and electronic)

© Pearson Education Limited 2013 (print and electronic)

The right of John A. Kirk to be identified as author of this work has been asserted by him in accordance with the Copyright, Designs and Patents Act 1988.

Pearson Education is not responsible for the content of third-party internet sites.

ISBN: 978-1-4082-2013-9 (print)
    978-0-273-78023-6 (PDF)

British Library Cataloguing-in-Publication Data
A catalogue record for the print edition is available from the British Library

Library of Congress Cataloging-in-Publication Data
Kirk, John A., 1970–
    Martin Luther King and the civil rights movement / John A. Kirk.
        pages cm. – (Seminar studies)
    Includes index.
    ISBN 978-1-4082-2013-9 (pbk.)
    1. King, Martin Luther, Jr., 1929–1968.   2. African Americans–Civil rights–History–20th century.   3. Civil rights movements–United States–History–20th century.   I. Title.
    E185.97.K5K57 2013
    323.092–dc23
    [B]
                                                                            2012049193

10 9 8 7 6 5 4 3 2 1
17 16 15 14 13

Cover image © Getty Images

Print edition typeset in 10/13.5pt ITC Berkeley by 35
Print edition printed and bound in Malaysia, CTP-KHL

NOTE THAT ANY PAGE CROSS REFERENCES REFER TO THE PRINT EDITION

Introduction to the series

History is narrative constructed by historians from traces left by the past. Historical enquiry is often driven by contemporary issues and, in consequence, historical narratives are constantly reconsidered, reconstructed and reshaped. The fact that different historians have different perspectives on issues means that there is also often controversy and no universally agreed version of past events. *Seminar Studies* was designed to bridge the gap between current research and debate, and the broad, popular general surveys that often date rapidly.

The volumes in the series are written by historians who are not only familiar with the latest research and current debates concerning their topic, but who have themselves contributed to our understanding of the subject. The books are intended to provide the reader with a clear introduction to a major topic in history. They provide both a narrative of events and a critical analysis of contemporary interpretations. They include the kinds of tools generally omitted from specialist monographs: a chronology of events, a glossary of terms and brief biographies of 'who's who'. They also include bibliographical essays in order to guide students to the literature on various aspects of the subject. Students and teachers alike will find that the selection of documents will stimulate discussion and offer insight into the raw materials used by historians in their attempt to understand the past.

Clive Emsley and Gordon Martel
Series Editors

Contents

Author's acknowledgements

The making of this book has stretched over a decade and three different employers. It is a substantially revised, reorganized and updated version of my earlier *Martin Luther King, Jr.* volume that appeared in Pearson Longman's *Profiles in Power* series in 2005. That project began when series editor Keith Robbins, who was principal at the University of Wales, Lampeter, at the time, suggested I write the King book when I was a lecturer in the History Department there. Heather McCallum oversaw much of the editorial work on that project. I completed the book while in the History Department at Royal Holloway, University of London, where I moved in 1999. In 2009, Christina Wipf Perry at Pearson Longman suggested converting the book into a format suitable for the *Seminar Studies* series. One transatlantic move later, to the University of Arkansas at Little Rock (UALR), in 2010, and the book was soon(ish) thereafter finished. At Pearson Longman, Mari Shullaw and Sarah Turpie have overseen the project to completion. Finishing the book in Little Rock, Arkansas, which was home to one of the major flash-points of the civil rights movement in September 1957, when President Dwight D. Eisenhower sent federal troops to the city to desegregate Central High School, has been a fitting backdrop to the end of the journey.

The launch of UALR's Institute on Race and Ethnicity in the summer of 2011 staked its claim to be the 'keeper of the flame' on race relations in the city. The institute, driven by a sense of personal mission by UALR Chancellor Joel Anderson, and the regular weekly meetings of the Chancellor's Committee on Race and Ethnicity every Monday during semester time, has provided a stimulating and nurturing environment for my work. I would like to thank everyone on the committee – with its members drawn from right across the university and who give their time voluntarily to participate – for their insights and dedication. The other big change in the last decade alongside the various job moves is the birth of my daughter, Sadie. My earlier *Profiles in Power* book was dedicated to my wife, Charlene. Now I can dedicate this book to both of the ladies in my life, who, though they are probably guilty of stretching out its completion for longer than it should have taken, have made that time much more enjoyable too.

Publisher's acknowledgements

We are grateful to the following for permission to reproduce copyright material.

Documents
Document 9 is a 1961 Herb Block Cartoon, © The Herb Block Foundation; Document 10 from an Interview with Albany Police Chief, Laurie Pritchett, 23 April 1976 (B-0027), in the Southern Oral History Program Collection (#4007), Southern Historical Collection, Louis Round Wilson Special Collections Library, University of North Carolina at Chapel Hill; Document 12 from *Malcolm X Speaks*, by Malcolm X, published by Pathfinder Press in 1989, Copyright © 1965, 1989 by Betty Shabazz and Pathfinder Press. Reprinted by permission; Document 14 from Eidenmuller, M. E., *Great Speeches for Better Speaking* © 2008, McGraw-Hill. Reproduced with the permission of The McGraw-Hill Companies;

Maps
Map of key events in the civil rights movement, from Boyer. *Promises to Keep*, 3E. © 2005 Wadsworth, a part of Cengage Learning, Inc. Reproduced by permission. www.cengage.com/permissions.

Picture Credits
The publisher would like to thank the following for their kind permission to reproduce their photographs:

Plate 1: Pictorial Press Ltd / Alamy; Plates 2, 4, 5 and 6: Bettman / Corbis; Plate 3: Flip Schulke/CORBIS.

All other images © Pearson Education

In some instances we have been unable to trace the owners of copyright material, and we would appreciate any information that would enable us to do so.

Abbreviations

ACHR	Alabama Council on Human Relations
ACMHR	Alabama Christian Movement for Human Rights
AFSCME	American Federation of State, County and Municipal Employees
ASWPL	Association of Southern Women for the Prevention of Lynching
BSCPU	Brotherhood of Sleeping Car Porters Union
CCCO	Coordinating Council of Community Organizations
CFM	Chicago Freedom Movement
CIC	Commission on Interracial Cooperation
COFO	Council of Federated Organizations
COME	Community on the Move for Equality
CORE	Congress of Racial Equality
CRS	Community Relations Service
CUCRL	Council for United Civil Rights Leadership
DCVL	Dallas County Voters League
EOA	Economic Opportunity Act
FBI	Federal Bureau of Investigation
FEPC	Fair Employment Practices Committee
FOR	Fellowship of Reconciliation
FRCC	Freedom Rides Coordinating Committee
HBUC	Historically Black Universities and Colleges
ICC	Interstate Commerce Commission
KKK	Ku Klux Klan
MFDP	Mississippi Freedom Democratic Party
MIA	Montgomery Improvement Association
MOWM	March on Washington Movement

NAACP	National Association for the Advancement of Colored People
NUL	National Urban League
NOI	Nation of Islam
OEO	Office of Economic Opportunity
PPC	Poor People's Campaign
SCLC	Southern Christian Leadership Conference
SNCC	Student Nonviolent Coordinating Committee
SRC	Southern Regional Council
UAW	United Auto Workers
UNIA	Universal Negro Improvement Association
WPC	Women's Political Council

Chronology

1865

18 December Thirteenth Amendment outlaws slavery

1868

28 July Fourteenth Amendment promises 'equal protection under the law'

1870

30 March Fifteenth Amendment promises the vote without consideration of 'race, color, or previous condition of servitude'

1896

6 May US Supreme Court upholds the legal doctrine of 'separate but equal' in *Plessy v. Ferguson*

1898

25 April US Supreme Court upholds use of poll tax and literacy tests as voter qualifications in *Williams v. Mississippi*

1909

1 June National Association for the Advancement of Colored People founded

1915

21 June *Guinn v. US* outlaws use of the 'grandfather clause' to prevent black voting

1929

15 January Martin Luther King, Jr. is born in Atlanta, Georgia

1941

June A. Philip Randolph's threat of a March on Washington Movement leads President Franklin D. Roosevelt to pass federal fair employment legislation

1942

3 August   Congress of Racial Equality founded in Chicago

1944

3 April   *Smith* v. *Allwright* outlaws all-white Democratic Party primary elections

20 September   King enters Morehouse College in Atlanta, Georgia

1946

3 June   *Morgan* v. *Virginia* outlaws segregated seating on interstate buses

1947

9 April   CORE embarks on a 'Journey of Reconciliation' to test the *Morgan* ruling

1948

25 February   King is ordained by his father at Ebenezer Baptist Church

8 June   King graduates from Morehouse College with a BA degree in sociology

26 July   President Harry S. Truman issues Executive Order 9981 leading to the desegregation of the armed services

14 September   King enters Crozer Theological Seminary in Chester, Pennsylvania

1951

May   King graduates from Crozer Theological Seminary with a divinity degree

13 September   King enters Boston University to study for a PhD in systematic theology

1953

18 June   King and Coretta Scott King are married in Marion, Alabama

1954

17 May   *Brown* v. *Board of Education* outlaws segregation in schools

1 September   King begins his first job as pastor at Dexter Avenue Baptist Church

1955

31 May   Brown implementation order (*Brown II*) calls for desegregation 'with all deliberate speed'

5 June   King graduates from Boston University with a PhD in systematic theology

28 August   Emmett Till is killed

17 November   The Kings' first child, Yolanda Denise, is born

1 December   Rosa Parks is arrested, leading to the Montgomery bus boycott

5 December   A mass meeting at Holt Baptist Church votes to form the Montgomery Improvement Association (MIA). King becomes president

1956

27 January	King experiences a spiritual revelation in prayer that gives him the strength to continue as leader of the bus boycott
30 January	The Kings' home is bombed by whites
12 March	101 southern congressmen sign the 'Southern Manifesto' declaring the *Brown* ruling unconstitutional
13 November	US Supreme Court rules bus segregation laws in Montgomery and Alabama unconstitutional
21 December	King is one of the first people to ride desegregated buses in Montgomery

1957

14 February	Southern Christian Leadership Conference is founded
6 March	King attends Ghanaian independence celebrations in Africa
17 May	King delivers 'Give Us the Ballot' speech at the 'Prayer Pilgrimage for Freedom,' Lincoln Memorial, Washington DC
29 August	1957 Civil Rights Bill passes into law
24 September	Little Rock school crisis leads to President Dwight D. Eisenhower sending federal troops to Arkansas's capital city to desegregate Central High School
23 October	The Kings' second child, Martin III, is born

1958

17 September	King's first book *Stride Toward Freedom: The Montgomery Story* is published
20 September	King is stabbed by Izola Ware Curry at a book signing in Harlem, New York

1960

1 February	King moves from Montgomery to Atlanta to become assistant pastor at his father's Ebenezer Baptist Church; sit-in movement begins in Greensboro, North Carolina
17 April	Student Nonviolent Coordinating Committee is founded
19 October	King is arrested at a sit-in demonstration at Rich's department store in Atlanta
5 December	*Boynton* v. *Virginia* outlaws segregation in interstate bus terminals

1961

31 January	The Kings' third child, Dexter Scott, is born
4 May	CORE 'Freedom Ride' begins
21 May	A mob besieges a church meeting in Montgomery after Freedom Riders arrive in the city

22 September	Interstate Commerce Commission bans segregation on interstate buses effective from 1 November
November–December	The Albany Campaign begins
16 December	King and Ralph Abernathy are arrested in Albany

1962

1 October	James Meredith desegregates the University of Mississippi

1963

March–June	The Birmingham Campaign
28 March	The Kings' fourth child, Bernice Albertine, is born
16 April	King writes 'Letter from Birmingham City Jail'
7 May	Demonstrators are attacked by police dogs and spray from high-powered fire hoses in Birmingham
11 June	President John F. Kennedy addresses the nation on television and calls civil rights a 'moral issue'
12 June	NAACP field secretary Medgar Evers is killed
28 August	King delivers 'I Have a Dream' speech at the March on Washington
18 September	King delivers eulogy at the funeral for three of the four girls killed in the Sixteenth Street Church bombing on 15 September
10 October	US Attorney General authorizes the FBI to wiretap King's home phone
22 November	President John F. Kennedy is killed in Dallas, Texas

1964

23 January	Twenty-Fourth Amendment to the US Constitution outlaws the poll tax
March–June	The St Augustine Campaign
26 April	Mississippi Freedom Democratic Party (MFDP) is founded
21 June	James Chaney, Andrew Goodman and Michael Schwerner are killed in Mississippi
2 July	Civil Rights Act of 1964 signed into law by President Lyndon B. Johnson
August	Democratic National Convention in Atlantic City, New Jersey
18 November	FBI director J. Edgar Hoover labels King 'the most notorious liar in the country'
10 December	King receives the Nobel Peace Prize in Oslo, Norway

1965

January–March	The Selma Campaign
18 February	Jimmie Lee Jackson is shot in Perry County, Alabama. Dies 26 February, the first fatality in an SCLC campaign

21 February	Malcolm X is killed in New York
7 March	'Bloody Sunday' in Selma: marchers are gassed and beaten by state troopers
21 March	Selma to Montgomery march begins
6 August	Voting Rights Act of 1965 signed into law by President Johnson
11–16 August	Race riots erupt in Watts, Los Angeles

1966

26 January	The King family moves into a Chicago apartment at 1550 South Hamlin Avenue
6 June	James Meredith shot on his 'March Against Fear'
10 June	Stokely Carmichael popularizes the 'Black Power' slogan
10 July	The Chicago Campaign 'Open Housing' marches begin
1 October	Black Panther Party organizes in Oakland, California

1967

4 April	King delivers 'Beyond Vietnam – A Time to Break Silence' speech at New York's Riverside Church
1 September	Thurgood Marshall appointed first black US Supreme Court Justice
7 November	Carl Stokes elected first black mayor of a major city in Cleveland, Ohio
4 December	King publicly announces the Poor People's Campaign

1968

29 February	Kerner Commission Report warns US is 'moving toward two societies, one black, one white – separate and unequal'
28 March	King leads a march in support of striking Memphis sanitation workers that descends into violence and looting
3 April	King delivers 'I've Been to the Mountaintop' speech at Mason Temple in Memphis
4 April	King is killed by a sniper's bullet on the balcony of the Lorraine Motel in Memphis
9 April	King is buried in Atlanta
11 April	Fair Housing Act is signed into law by President Johnson
May–June	The Poor People's Campaign

1984

Fall	Jesse Jackson becomes first serious contender for black presidential candidate

1986

20 January   First Martin Luther King, Jr. Day federal holiday

1989

7 November   L. Douglas Wilder becomes first US elected black governor in Virginia

1995

16 October   Nation of Islam leader Louis Farrakhan organizes Million Man March in Washington DC

2008

4 November   Barack Obama is elected first black president of the United States

Who's who

Abernathy, Ralph D. (1926–1990): Montgomery, Alabama, minister who became one of King's closest confidants in the SCLC and succeeded King as SCLC president in 1968.

Ali, Muhammad (1942–): Three times world heavyweight champion boxer, Cassius Clay changed his name to Muhammad Ali after joining the NOI in 1964.

Ames, Jesse Daniel (1883–1972): White southern woman who founded the Association of Southern Women for the Prevention of Lynching in 1930.

Anderson, Dr William G. (1927–): Physician and educator who served as president of the Albany Movement 1961–1962.

Baker, Ella (1903–1986): Director of NAACP branches in the 1940s and instrumental in the founding of the SCLC and SNCC.

Baker, Wilson (1915–1975): Director of public safety in Selma, Alabama, during the SCLC's Selma Campaign.

Barry, Marion (1936–): First chair of SNCC and later active in Washington DC politics, including four terms as mayor.

Belafonte, Harry (1927–): Famous black singer, songwriter and actor, who played many benefit concerts to support the civil rights movement.

Bethune, Mary McLeod (1875–1955): Educator, activist, president of the National Association of Colored Women, and founder of the National Council of Negro Women.

Bevel, James (1936–2008): Recruited from the student sit-in movement in Nashville to become one of the SCLC's most innovative and influential tacticians.

Blair, Ezell, Jr. (1941–): Since 1968 Jibreel Khazan, one of the Greensboro Four students to stage the first sit-ins in Greensboro, North Carolina.

Blake, J. Fred (1912–2002): Bus driver in Montgomery, Alabama. Rosa Parks's refusal to give up her seat at his request led to the Montgomery bus boycott.

Bond, Julian (1940–): A founder member of SNCC and its communications director 1961–1966.

Boutwell, Albert (1904–78): Mayor of Birmingham, Alabama, during the SCLC's Birmingham Campaign.

Boynton, Amelia Platts (1911–): One of the leading local figures in the 1965 Selma Campaign.

Brightman, Dr Edgar S. (1884–1953): Professor at Boston University who was influential in the philosophy of personalism, a belief in the importance and worth of an individual's actions.

Brown, Bailey (1917–2004): Federal District judge who issued an injunction against civil rights movement marches taking place in Memphis in 1968.

Carmichael, Stokely (1941–1998): Freedom Rider and sit-in demonstrator who became chair of SNCC in 1966 and popularized the Black Power slogan on the Meredith March Against Fear.

Chaney, James (1943–1964): Black Mississippian who was killed during Freedom Summer along with white activists Andrew Goodman and Michael Schwerner.

Clark, James G., Jr. (1922–2007): Segregationist sheriff of Selma, Alabama, whose heavy-handed policing methods brought national attention during the Selma Campaign.

Collins, Addie Mae (1949–1963): One of four black girls killed at the bombing of Birmingham, Alabama, Sixteenth Street Baptist Church in September 1963.

Collins, LeRoy (1909–1991): Governor of Florida (1955–1961) who was appointed by President Johnson as director of the Community Relations Service in 1964.

Colvin, Claudette (1939–): Arrested in Montgomery, Alabama, for breaking segregation ordinance on a city bus in 1955, nine months before Rosa Parks.

Connor, Theophilus Eugene 'Bull' (1897–1973): Public safety commissioner in Birmingham, Alabama, whose policing of 1961 Freedom Rides and the 1963 Birmingham Campaign brought the civil rights movement national attention.

Curry, Izola Ware (1916–): Stabbed King in the chest with a letter opener at a book signing in Harlem, New York, in 1958. She was subsequently committed to a mental institution.

Daley, Richard J. (1902–1976): Mayor of Chicago (1955–1976), he supported the civil rights movement in the South, but proved more reticent to do so during the SCLC's 1965–1966 Chicago Campaign.

Delaney, Martin (1812–1885): Civil War soldier, journalist, physician and an early advocate of black nationalism.

DeWolf, L. Harold (1905–1986): King's PhD dissertation adviser at Boston University.

Doar, John (1921–): Assistant Attorney General for Civil Rights in the US Department of Justice 1960–1967.

Dolan, Joseph F. (1921–2008): Assistant Deputy Attorney General (1960–1965) who helped to broker the Birmingham Truce Agreement in 1963.

Du Bois, W. E. B. (1868–1963): First black Harvard PhD, founder member of the NAACP, and editor of its newspaper *The Crisis*.

Durr, Virginia (1903–1999): Along with her husband, lawyer Clifford Durr, one of the few white supporters of the civil rights movement in Montgomery, Alabama.

Eisenhower, Dwight D. (1890–1969): Thirty-fourth president of the United States (Republican) 1953–1961, who sent federal troops to Little Rock, Arkansas, in September 1957 to desegregate Central High School.

Elliott, J. Robert (1910–2006): Federal District judge who issued an injunction against civil rights marches in Albany, Georgia, in 1962.

Eskridge, Chauncey (1917–1988): SCLC general counsel in the late 1960s who represented King in his last case, removing an injunction against marching in Memphis, Tennessee.

Evers, Charles (1922–): Mississippi NAACP field secretary and older brother of slain civil rights leader Medgar Evers.

Evers, Medgar (1925–1963): Mississippi NAACP field secretary who was killed by segregationist Byron De La Beckwith in 1963.

Farmer, James L., Jr. (1920–1999): Co-founder of CORE and its national chair 1942–1944 and national director 1961–1965.

Forman, James (1928–2005): Executive secretary of SNCC 1961–1965.

Gandhi, Mohandas K. (1869–1948): Indian Independence leader whose practice of non-violent civil disobedience was influential on the thought and tactics of King and the civil rights movement.

Garvey, Marcus (1887–1940): Jamaican political leader who founded the UNIA and built the first mass black movement in the United States in the 1920s.

Goldwater, Barry (1909–1998): Republican presidential nominee for the 1964 election who ran on an anti-civil rights ticket.

Goodman, Andrew (1943–1964): White New Yorker who was killed during the 1964 Mississippi Freedom Summer along with fellow activists James Chaney and Michael Schwerner.

Gray, Fred D. (1930–): Montgomery, Alabama, attorney who represented Rosa Parks and King during the Montgomery bus boycott and argued many landmark cases in his home state.

Green, Edith (1910–1987): Chair of the Credentials Committee at the 1964 Democratic National Convention that refused to seat MFDP delegates.

Hamer, Fannie Lou (1917–1977): Grassroots civil rights leader from Mississippi who co-founded the MFDP and was its vice-chair at the 1964 Democratic National Convention.

Hegel, G. W. (1770–1831): German philosopher whose dialectic method of analysis, which sought to reconcile opposite points of view, influenced King.

Henry, Aaron (1922–1997): President of the Mississippi State Conference of NAACP branches, a founder of the MFDP and COFO, and MFDP chair at the 1964 Democratic National Convention.

Hollowell, Donald L. (1917–2004): Atlanta-based civil rights attorney who got King released from prison after his sit-in conviction in 1960.

Hoover, J. Edgar (1895–1972): Director of the FBI (1935–1972) who was complicit in the harassment of King and others in the civil rights movement.

Houston, Charles Hamilton (1895–1950): NAACP attorney who formulated a legal strategy for dismantling segregation through the courts in the 1930s.

Humphrey, Hubert (1911–1978): Lyndon B. Johnson's vice president (1965–1969) and an important intermediary between Johnson and the MFDP at the 1964 Democratic National Convention.

Jackson, Jesse (1941–): Greenville, South Carolina, native who was involved in the Greensboro, North Carolina, sit-ins and with SCLC's Operation Breadbasket in Chicago.

Jackson, Jimmie Lee (1938–1965): Killed by an Alabama state trooper in Marion, Perry County, his death prompted the Selma to Montgomery march.

Jemison, Theodore J. (1918–): Leader of the 1953 Baton Rouge, Louisiana, bus boycott and a founder member of the SCLC.

Johns, Vernon (1892–1965): Activist minister in Montgomery, Alabama, who was fired as pastor of Dexter Avenue Baptist Church for being too outspoken and was replaced by Martin Luther King, Jr.

Johnson, Frank M. (1918–1999): Pro-civil rights Alabama federal judge who ruled in favour of desegregation of Montgomery buses and upheld the Selma to Montgomery march.

Johnson, Lyndon B. (1908–1973): Thirty-sixth president of the United States (Democrat) 1963–1969, who was instrumental in the passage of the Civil Rights Act of 1964 and the Voting Rights Act of 1965, and the architect of plans for a Great Society.

Katzenbach, Nicholas (1922–2012): Deputy Attorney General in the Kennedy administration (1962–1965) and Attorney General in the Johnson administration (1965–1966).

Kelley, Asa D. (1922–1997): Albany mayor during King's 1961–1962 Albany Campaign and a defender of segregation.

Kennedy, John F. (1917–1963): Thirty-fifth president of the United States (Democrat) 1961–1963 who gradually moved in support of the civil rights movement before he was assassinated in November 1963.

Kennedy, Robert (1925–1968): US Attorney General (1961–1964) who handled much of his brother John F. Kennedy's civil rights policy and became a strong supporter of the movement by the time of his assassination in June 1968.

Kerner, Otto (1908–1976): Governor of Illinois (1961–1968) who chaired the National Advisory Commission on Civil Disorders (also known as the Kerner Commission).

King, Alberta Williams (1904–1974): Mother of Martin Luther King, Jr.

King, Alfred Daniel Williams (1930–1969): Better known as A. D. King, Martin Luther King's younger brother was a Baptist minister in Birmingham, Alabama.

King, Bernice Albertine (1963–): Youngest child of Martin Luther King, Jr. and Coretta Scott King.

King, Christine (1927–): Elder sister of Martin Luther King, Jr.

King, Coretta Scott (1927–2006): Wife of Martin Luther King, Jr. who became increasingly involved in human rights activism after her husband's death.

King, Dexter Scott (1961–): Third child of Martin Luther King, Jr. and Coretta Scott King.

King, Martin Luther King III (1957–): Second child of Martin Luther King, Jr. and Coretta Scott King.

King, Jr., Martin Luther (1929–1968): President of the SCLC (1957–1968) and America's most prominent and popular civil rights movement leader in the late 1950s and 1960s.

King, Sr., Martin Luther (1899–1984): Better known as Daddy King, he was the father of Martin Luther King, Jr., a Baptist minister, and an early civil rights leader in Atlanta.

King, Yolanda Denise (1955–2007): Eldest child of Martin Luther King, Jr. and Coretta Scott King.

Kyles, Billy (1934–): Baptist minister involved in the 1968 Memphis sanitation workers strike.

Lawson, James (1928–): Member of FOR and CORE who was an innovative tactician, practitioner and teacher of non-violence.

Lee, Bernard (1935–1991): SCLC field secretary who was a close personal assistant to and constant travelling companion of Martin Luther King, Jr.

Levison, Stanley (1912–1979): Jewish New York businessman who helped to found the SCLC and remained a close friend and adviser to Martin Luther King, Jr.

Lewis, John (1940–): One of the original 1961 Freedom Riders, SNCC chair 1963–1966, and a participant in many of the major civil rights campaigns of the 1960s. Since 1987 he has been a US congressman for Georgia's 5th District.

Lincoln, Abraham (1809–1865): Sixteenth president of the United States (Republican) 1861–1865 whose 1863 Emancipation Proclamation marked the beginning of the end of slavery in the South.

Liuzzo, Viola Gregg (1925–1965): White woman activist killed by the Ku Klux Klan while driving home participants from the Selma to Montgomery march.

Loeb, Henry (1920–1992): Memphis mayor during the 1968 sanitation workers strike.

Marshall, Burke (1922–2003): Head of the Civil Rights Division of the US Department of Justice 1961–1964.

Marshall, Thurgood (1908–1993): NAACP attorney who argued many landmark civil rights cases and who was the first black appointment to the US Supreme Court by President Johnson, serving 1967–1991.

Marx, Karl (1818–1883): German philosopher and communist advocate. Although King was not a Marxist, Marx influenced King's view of the world from his college studies until his assassination.

Mays, Benjamin E. (1894–1984): Minister, educator, scholar and activist who was president of Morehouse College in Atlanta, Georgia, from 1940–1967.

McCain, Franklin (1941–): One of the Greensboro Four students to stage the first sit-ins in Greensboro, North Carolina.

McCarthy, Joseph T. (1908–1957): Wisconsin senator whose claims of communist infiltration in the US drove anti-communist hysteria in the 1950s.

McKissick, Floyd (1922–1991): CORE national director (1966–1968) who as a Black Power supporter led the organization in a more militant direction.

McNair, Denise (1951–1963): One of four black girls killed at the bombing of Birmingham, Alabama, Sixteenth Street Baptist Church in September 1963.

Meredith, James (1933–): First black student admitted to the University of Mississippi (Ole Miss) in October 1962 and who instigated a March Against Fear across Mississippi in 1966.

Minh, Ho Chi (1890–1969): President of pro-communist Democratic Republic of Vietnam (1955–1969) during the Vietnam War.

Moody, Anne (1940–): Mississippi activist whose autobiography *Coming of Age in Mississippi* (1968) provides a vivid account of black rural life and activism in the state.

Nash, Diane (1938–): One of the influential Nashville group of sit-in students who helped to found SNCC, participated in the 1961 Freedom Rides, and later worked for the SCLC.

Nixon, Edgar Daniel (1899–1987): Better known as E. D. Nixon, who was head of the BSCPU branch in Montgomery, Alabama, and one of the key organizers of the Montgomery bus boycott.

Nixon, Richard M. (1913–1994): Thirty-seventh president of the United States (Republican) 1969–1974 and thirty-sixth vice president of the United States (under Eisenhower) 1953–1961.

Page, Marion S. (1896–1971): Black postal worker in Albany, Georgia, who was one of the leaders of the Albany Movement.

Parks, Rosa L. (1913–2005): Civil rights activist whose refusal to surrender her seat on a Montgomery, Alabama, bus led to the Montgomery bus boycott.

Pastore, John (1907–2000): Governor of Rhode Island (1945–1950), senator (1950–1976), and chair of the 1964 Democratic National Convention.

Patterson, John Malcolm (1921–): Governor of Alabama (1959–1963) who failed to deliver on his promise to protect Freedom Riders in the state.

Peck, James (1914–1993): The only white person to participate in both the 1947 Journey of Reconciliation and the 1961 Freedom Ride.

Price, Cecil Ray (1938–2001): Deputy sheriff in Neshoba County, Mississippi, linked to the murders of Chaney, Goodman and Schwerner in 1964 and who was convicted of violating their civil rights in 1967 and served four and a half years in prison.

Pritchett, Laurie (1926–2000): Chief of police in Albany, Georgia, during the 1961–1962 Albany Campaign.

Raby, Albert (1933–1988): Founder of the Chicago's CCCO in 1962 and co-chair of the Chicago Movement 1965–1966.

Randolph, A. Philip (1889–1979): Organized the BSCPU in 1925 and served as its president 1925–1968.

Rauchenbush, Walter (1861–1918): Theologian and Baptist minister who advocated a Social Gospel of church engagement and activism in social issues.

Rauh, Joseph L., Jr. (1911–1992): Civil rights and civil liberties attorney who represented the MFDP at the 1964 Democratic Party Convention.

Reagon, Cordell (1943–1996): SNCC leader in the Albany Movement.

Reddick, Lawrence D. (1910–1995): Black historian at Alabama State College who knew Martin Luther King, Jr., travelled with him, and wrote King's earliest biography in 1958.

Reeb, James B. (1927–1965): White Boston minister killed by local whites during the Selma Campaign.

Reuther, Walter (1907–1970): President of the United Auto Workers and one of the civil rights movement's strongest allies in the labour movement.

Richmond, David (1941–1990): One of the Greensboro Four students to stage the first sit-ins in Greensboro, North Carolina.

Ricks, Willie (1943–): SNCC field secretary also known as Mukasa Dada who was first to use the Black Power slogan on the 1966 Meredith March Against Fear.

Robertson, Carole (1949–1963): One of four black girls killed at the bombing of Birmingham, Alabama, Sixteenth Street Baptist Church in September 1963.

Robinson, Jo Ann (1912–1992): Montgomery, Alabama, teacher, head of the Woman's Political Council, and a key organizer of the Montgomery bus boycott.

Roosevelt, Franklin D. (1882–1945): Thirty-second president of the United States (Democrat) 1933–1945 who was the architect of the New Deal that sought to pull the US out of economic Depression in the 1930s.

Rowan, Carl T. (1925–2000): One of the most prominent black journalists of the twentieth century who served in both the Kennedy and Johnson presidential administrations.

Rustin, Bayard (1912–1987): Movement strategist and non-violence advocate who belonged to FOR, helped organize the 1941 March on Washington Movement and the 1963 March on Washington, participated in the 1947 Journey of Reconciliation, and was crucial in the founding of the SCLC.

Schwerner, Michael (1939–1964): White New Yorker who was killed during the 1964 Mississippi Freedom Summer along with fellow activists James Chaney and Andrew Goodman.

Sellers, Clyde C. (1908–1976): Police commissioner in Montgomery during the 1955–1956 bus boycott.

Sherrod, Charles (1937–): SNCC field secretary and later director of SNCC in south-west Georgia who helped to found the Albany Movement.

Shuttlesworth, Fred (1922–2011): Baptist minister in Birmingham, Alabama, who was a co-founder of the SCLC and the founder of the ACMHR.

Siegenthaler, John (1927–): Robert Kennedy's administrative assistant (1960–1961) who was chief negotiator for the Kennedy administration during the 1961 Freedom Rides.

Smith, Lillian (1897–1966): White woman activist and writer who was a friend of the Kings.

Smitherman, Joseph (1929–2005): Mayor of Selma, Alabama, during the Selma Campaign.

Spock, Benjamin Dr (1903–1998): Paediatrician and social activist who supported the civil rights and anti-Vietnam War movements.

Steele, C. Kenzie (1914–1980): Baptist minister who organized the Tallahassee bus boycott in 1956 and who was a member of the SCLC.

Sullivan, William C. (1912–1977): Director of the FBI's intelligence division 1961–1971.

Thurmond, Strom (1902–2003): South Carolina senator and long-standing opponent to civil rights in Congress.

Tilley, John L. (1898–1971): Baptist minister and SCLC executive secretary 1958–1959.

Truman, Harry S. (1884–1972): Thirty-third president of the United States (Democrat) 1945–1953 who issued Executive Order 9981 to desegregate the US armed forces.

Turner, Henry McNeal (1834–1915): African Methodist Episcopalian bishop who was an early advocate of black nationalism and emigration to Africa in the late nineteenth century.

Vivian, Cordy Tindell (1924–): Better known as C. T. Vivian, he was a Baptist minster, a member of the SCLC's executive committee, and a close friend of King.

Walker, Wyatt T. (1929–): Baptist minister and executive director of the SCLC 1960–1964.

Wallace, George (1919–1998): Infamous pro-segregation Alabama governor 1963–1967, 1971–1979, and 1983–1987.

Washington, Booker T. (1856–1915): Black America's chief spokesperson in the late nineteenth and early twentieth centuries who founded Tuskegee Institute in Alabama.

Webb, Sheyann (1956–): At eight years old she was King's 'smallest freedom fighter' in the 1965 Selma Campaign.

Wells, Ida B. (1862–1931): Memphis journalist and anti-lynching crusader.

Wesley, Cynthia (1949–1963): One of four black girls killed at the bombing of Birmingham, Alabama, Sixteenth Street Baptist Church in September 1963.

Wilkins, Roy (1901–1981): Executive secretary of the NAACP (1955–1964) and executive director (1964–1977).

Williams, Adam Daniel (1861–1931): Maternal grandfather of Martin Luther King, Jr. who was born into slavery, became a Baptist minister, and was a founder member of the Atlanta branch of the NAACP.

Williams, Hosea (1926–2000): SCLC member and an organizer in a number of its campaigns.

X, Malcolm (1929–1965): Black Muslim minister and chief spokesperson for the Nation of Islam from the late 1950s to mid 1960s.

Young, Andrew (1932–): Baptist minister and executive director of the SCLC (1964–1970) who later served as Georgia congressman (1973–1977), US Ambassador to the United Nations (1977–1979), and mayor of Atlanta (1982–1990).

Young, Whitney (1921–1971): Executive director of the National Urban League 1961–1971.

Glossary of terms and organizations

Alabama Christian Movement for Human Rights: SCLC-affiliated civil rights organization headed by Rev. Fred Shuttlesworth.

Alabama Council on Human Relations: Interracial organization affiliated with the Southern Regional Council.

Albany Movement: A coalition of organizations that joined together to run the 1961–1962 Albany Campaign.

American Federation of State, County and Municipal Employees: Labour union that represents local and state government employees.

American Jewish Congress: Lobby group for Jewish interests, based in the United States.

Armed Self-Defence: Taking up weapons to prevent being attacked.

Association of Southern Women for the Prevention of Lynching: Founded by Jesse Daniel Ames in 1930 to petition, lobby and fundraise to prevent lynching.

Back-to-Africa: The idea that blacks are best served leaving the US and going back to Africa.

Baton Rouge Bus Boycott: A 1953 bus boycott in Louisiana that preceded the more famous 1955–1956 Montgomery bus boycott.

Big Six: The term used by the press to refer to the leaders of the 'Big Six' civil rights organizations: BSPCU, CORE, NAACP, NUL, SCLC and SNCC.

Black Muslims: An umbrella term for organizations promoting the interests of black Muslims, the most well known being the Nation of Islam.

Black Power: Slogan popularized by Stokely Carmichael in 1966 and often associated with black militancy, black nationalism and black armed self-defence.

Boynton v. Virginia (1960): US Supreme Court ruling that outlawed segregation in interstate bus terminals.

Brotherhood of Sleeping Car Porters Union: Labour union formed in 1925 to defend the interests of its predominantly black membership.

Browder v. Gayle (1956): US District Court case that led to the desegregation of buses in Montgomery.

Brown v. Board of Education (1954): Landmark US Supreme Court ruling that outlawed segregation in schools.

Chicago Freedom Movement: A coalition of organizations that joined together to run the 1965–1966 Chicago Campaign.

Civil Rights Act of 1957: First civil rights act since Reconstruction, which established the Department of Justice Civil Rights Division.

Civil Rights Act of 1964: Required the desegregation of public facilities and accommodations and a range of other pro-civil rights measures.

Cold War: A war of words and posturing, although rarely outright head-to-head conflict, fought between the US and Soviet Union between c. 1947 and 1991.

Commission on Interracial Cooperation: Formed in Atlanta in 1918 to help address southern racial problems and a forerunner of the Southern Regional Council.

Community on the Move for Equality: A Memphis coalition of striking workers and ministers formed to support the sanitation workers' strike.

Community Relations Service: Part of the Department of Justice formed by the 1964 Civil Rights Act to mediate community conflict.

Congress of Racial Equality: One of the 'Big Six' civil rights organizations, founded in 1942 and a pioneer in non-violent direct action.

Coordinating Council of Community Organizations: Local Chicago civil rights organization founded in 1962.

Council of Federated Organizations: A coalition of organizations that joined together to run the 1964 Mississippi Freedom Summer.

Council for United Civil Rights Leadership: Made up of the 'Big Six' civil rights organizations and formed to collect and distribute financial contributions to the civil rights movement.

Crusade for Citizenship: Early and largely unsuccessful SCLC voter registration campaign launched in 1958.

Dallas County Voters League: Local civic, civil rights and voting rights group founded in Selma, Alabama, in the late 1920s.

De Facto Segregation: Segregation that is enforced by or emerges from both formal and informal practices that are not explicitly sanctioned by law.

De Jure Segregation: Legally mandated segregation, such as the Jim Crow laws in southern states.

Deacons for Defense and Justice: Louisiana civil rights organization that advocated armed self-defence.

Democratic Party Credentials Committee: The committee charged with approving the credentials of all persons appointed or elected to the Democratic National Convention.

Double-V: Campaign launched by black newspaper the *Pittsburgh Courier* for victory against fascism abroad and racism in the US during World War II.

Economic Opportunity Act: The 1964 EOA was central to President Lyndon B. Johnson's Great Society and created a number of social programmes.

Emancipation Proclamation: 1863 Executive Order by President Abraham Lincoln that started the process of slave emancipation during the American Civil War.

Executive Order 8802: Issued by President Franklin D. Roosevelt, this forbade racial discrimination in wartime industry hiring practices and set up the Fair Employment Practices Committee to enforce the ban.

Executive Order 9981: Issued by President Harry S. Truman, this set in motion the process of desegregating the US armed forces.

Fair Employment Practices Committee: Created by President Franklin D. Roosevelt's Executive Order 8802 to monitor racial discrimination in federal hiring practices.

Federal Bureau of Investigation: The United States' federal criminal investigation and intelligence agency.

Filibuster: Talking at length to hold the floor of an assembly to prevent a vote from taking place.

Freedom Rides: Testing of desegregated bus terminals initiated by CORE in 1961.

Freedom Rides Coordinating Committee: A coalition of national civil rights organizations formed to orchestrate, coordinate and fund Freedom Rides over the summer of 1961.

Freedom Summer: A large-scale voter registration drive held in Mississippi in 1964.

Golgotha: According to the Bible, the place of Christ's crucifixion.

Great Migration: The population shift of blacks from the rural South to the urban North and West over the course of the twentieth century.

Great Society: The goal of a number of social programmes set in place by President Lyndon B. Johnson to improve the condition of marginalized groups in American society.

Harlem Renaissance: A flowering of black arts and culture in Harlem, New York, in the 1920s.

Interstate Commerce Commission: Federal body that regulates commerce and transportation between US states.

Jail not Bail: The tactic of remaining in jail rather than accepting bail as a form of protest.

Jim Crow: Named after a vaudeville character, the colloquial term given to southern segregation laws.

Journey of Reconciliation: Testing of desegregated interstate buses initiated by FOR in 1947.

Justice Department: The US Department of Justice is the federal executive department that enforces the law and administers justice.

Ku Klux Klan: White vigilante terror group formed at the end of the American Civil War.

Lynching: Extra-legal murder by two or more people of someone suspected of committing a crime.

March Against Fear: Instigated by James Meredith in 1966 as an individual protest to assert his right to free movement in the state, after his shooting it was continued with the support of all of the major civil rights organizations.

March on Washington for Jobs and Freedom: One of the largest civil rights gatherings of the 1960s with around 250,000 people participating at the Lincoln Memorial and Reflecting Pool in Washington DC.

March on Washington Movement: A 1941 movement designed to place pressure on the federal government to adopt fair employment practices during World War II.

Mississippi Freedom Democratic Party: A product of Freedom Summer, the MFDP demanded seats at the 1964 Democratic National Convention instead of the regular all-white delegation.

Montgomery Improvement Association: A coalition of organizations that joined together to run the 1955–1956 Montgomery bus boycott.

Morgan v. Virginia (1946): US Supreme Court ruling that outlawed segregation on interstate buses.

National Advisory Commission on Civil Disorders: Also known as the Kerner Commission after its chair Illinois governor Otto Kerner, the commission investigated the causes of the 'long hot summers' of racial unrest between 1965 and 1967.

National Association for the Advancement of Colored People: Founded in 1909 in New York, the NAACP is America's oldest civil rights organization and played a crucial role in laying the legal foundations for the civil rights movement in the 1940s and 1950s.

National Council of Negro Women: Black women's advocacy group founded by Mary McLeod Bethune in 1935.

National Urban League: Founded in 1910 in New York, the NUL focuses on providing social services and enhancing the economic conditions of urban blacks in America's largest cities.

Nation of Islam: Founded in 1930 in Detroit, the NOI is one of the most prominent Black Muslim groups in the United States.

New Deal: The collective name for a number of programmes and organizations created by the Franklin D. Roosevelt presidential administration to alleviate the effects of the Great Depression in the 1930s.

Nightriding: White vigilantism against and intimidation of black farmers.

Nobel Peace Prize: One of five distinguished Nobel Prizes awarded each year by the Norwegian Nobel Committee and won by Martin Luther King, Jr. in 1965.

Office of Economic Opportunity: Federal agency responsible for administering President Lyndon B. Johnson's Great Society programmes.

Operation Breadbasket: SCLC initiative from 1962 to 1972 that was dedicated to improving the economic conditions in black communities.

Personalism: A theological and philosophical belief in the importance and worth of an individual's actions.

Plessy v. Ferguson (1896): Landmark US Supreme Court decision that established the legal doctrine of 'separate but equal' and led to the expansion of segregation in southern states.

Poor People's Campaign: Martin Luther King, Jr.'s last campaign that focused on addressing issues of economic injustice.

Reconstruction: Period in US history from 1865 to 1877 following the American Civil War when Republicans tried to construct a biracial democracy in the South.

Redemption: Description by southerners of the period following Reconstruction when whites began to seize power and undermine the rights of freedmen.

Segregation: The enforced separation (sometimes legally mandated, sometimes not) of facilities and resources by race.

Senior Citizens Committee: A group of senior white businessmen that negotiated with civil rights representatives in the 1963 Birmingham Campaign.

Separate but Equal: The legal doctrine established in *Plessy* that said facilities for the races could be provided separately if they were of equal standard.

Sharecropping: An exploitative system of labour that often kept black farmers in debt to white landowners.

Sit-In: An act designed to directly challenge segregation laws and to force businesses to consider the economic viability of practising segregation.

Social Gospel: A movement and philosophy that applies Christian ethics to social problems.

Southern Christian Leadership Conference: A black minister-led civil rights organization founded in 1957 and headed by Martin Luther King, Jr. from 1957 to 1968.

Southern Manifesto: Document signed by 101 southern congressmen declaring the *Brown* decision unconstitutional.

Southern Regional Council: Atlanta-based interracial civil rights organization founded in 1944.

Spring Mobilization: A 1967 movement designed to bring together anti-war supporters in a push to withdraw US troops from Vietnam.

Student Nonviolent Coordinating Committee: A student-led civil rights organization that grew out of the 1960 sit-ins.

United Auto Workers: Labour union representing auto workers and one of the strongest labour movement supporters of civil rights.

Universal Negro Improvement Association: Founded by Jamaican Marcus Garvey in 1914, the black nationalist UNIA led the United States' earliest mass black movement in the 1920s.

Vietnam War: A war between the communist North Vietnam and the South Vietnamese regime which the US backed with political and military support from 1955 until its collapse in 1975.

Voting Rights Act of 1965: Act outlawing discriminatory voting practices such as literacy tests and establishing federal oversight of administering elections.

War on Poverty: The collective term for a number of social programmes set in place by President Lyndon B. Johnson to improve the conditions of marginalized groups in American society.

Whitecapping: Extra-legal enforcement of community values by secret societies that was often directed against blacks.

Williams v. Mississippi *(1898):* Landmark US Supreme Court decision that permitted the use of devices such as poll taxes and literacy tests that led to black disfranchisement.

Women's Political Council: Women's civil rights group in Montgomery, Alabama, headed by teacher Jo Ann Robinson, which played an important role in organizing the Montgomery bus boycott.

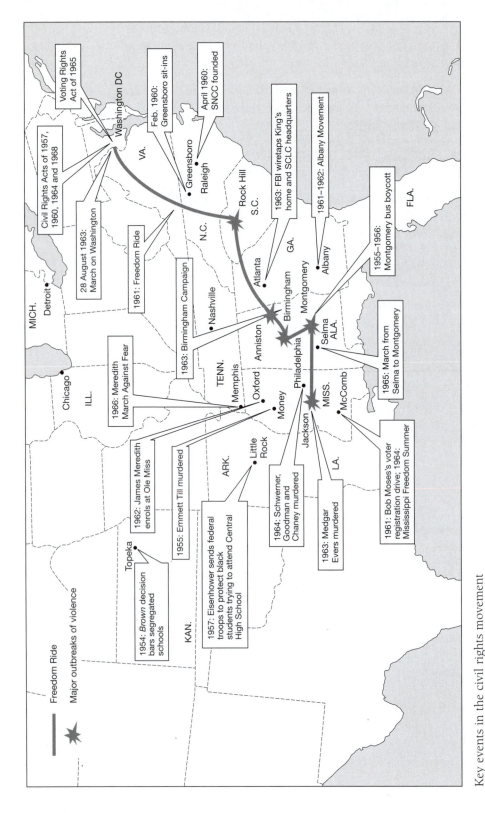

Key events in the civil rights movement

Source: Boyer, Paul S., *Promises to Keep* 3E. © 2005 Wadsworth, a part of Cengage Learning, Inc. Reproduced by permission.

Further reading and primary sources

FURTHER READING

The main purpose of this book is to provide a narrative analysis of King and the civil rights movement. For a more in-depth look at critical themes and debates see John A. Kirk, ed., *Martin Luther King, Jr. and the Civil Rights Movement: Controversies and Debates* (2007). There is an ever-growing selection of overviews on the black struggle for freedom and equality. Useful starting points are Robert Cook, *Sweet Land of Liberty: The African American Struggle for Civil Rights in the Twentieth Century* (1998); Adam Fairclough, *Better Day Coming: Blacks and Equality, 1890–2000* (2001); Steven F. Lawson, *Running For Freedom: Civil Rights and Black Politics Since 1941* (Third Edition, 2008); Manning Marable, *Race, Reform and Rebellion: The Second Reconstruction in Black America, 1945–1982* (Third Edition, 2007); Harvard Sitkoff, *The Struggle for Black Equality: The Emergence of Civil Rights as a National Issue* (Third Edition, 1981); and Stephen Tuck, *We Ain't What We Ought to Be: The Black Freedom Struggle from Emancipation to Obama* (2010).

PRIMARY SOURCES

The best web resource for King is the King Papers Project site at Stanford University, California http://mlk-kpp01.stanford.edu/index.php/kingpapers/index/ The King Papers Project is currently in the process of editing a 14-volume set of King's selected primary documents. At the time of writing, the first six volumes are available. The project has also made available King's own books in various editions: *Stride Toward Freedom: The Montgomery Story* (1958); *The Measure of a Man* (1959); *Strength to Love* (1963); *Why We Can't*

Wait (1964); *Where Do We Go From Here: Chaos or Community?* (1967); and *The Trumpet of Conscience* (1968).

There is a large amount of primary material on the civil rights movement available on the internet. One of the best repositories is Civil Rights Movement Veterans http://www.crmvet.org/ There are also a number of printed primary sources, including a wide selection of autobiographies and memoirs (see the Further Reading sections at the ends of chapters for more details). A good introduction to this literature is Kathy L. Nasstrom, 'Between Memory and History: Autobiographies of the Civil Rights Movement and the Writing of Civil Rights History', *Journal of Southern History* 74:2 (May 2008): 325–364.

Part 1

BACKGROUND

Introduction: Martin Luther King, Jr.: Saint, Sinner, or Historical Figure?

Early histories of the civil rights movement that appeared prior to the 1980s were purely biographies of Martin Luther King, Jr. Collectively, these works helped to create the familiar 'Montgomery to Memphis' narrative framework for understanding the history of the civil rights movement in the United States. This narrative begins with King's rise to leadership during the 1955 Montgomery bus boycott in Alabama, and ends with his 1968 assassination in Memphis, Tennessee.

Since the 1980s, a number of studies examining the civil rights movement at local and state levels have questioned the usefulness and accuracy of the King-centred Montgomery to Memphis narrative as the sole way of understanding the movement. These studies have made it clear that civil rights struggles already existed in many of the communities where King and the organization that he was president of, the **Southern Christian Leadership Conference (SCLC)**, ran civil rights campaigns in the 1960s. Moreover, those struggles continued long after King and the SCLC had left those communities. Civil rights activism also thrived in many places that King and the SCLC never even visited.

The historiography of Martin Luther King, Jr. and the civil rights movement, as that term itself implies, has consequently developed in two distinct strands. The literature is made up, on the one hand of biographies of King in the 'Montgomery to Memphis' mould, and on the other of histories of the civil rights movement that have increasingly tended to frame that movement within the context of a much larger, ongoing struggle for black freedom and equality unfolding in the twentieth century at local, state, national and even international levels.

Southern Christian Leadership Conference: A black minister-led civil rights organization founded in 1957 and headed by Martin Luther King, Jr. from 1957 to 1968.

Partisan movement activists have played their own role in reinforcing the idea that there is a division between the 'man and the movement'. Notably, there is the over-used quote from Ella Baker, a former SCLC staff member, who, disillusioned with the organization and King, went on to become instrumental in the formation of the **Student Nonviolent Coordinating Committee (SNCC)**, that 'The movement made Martin rather than Martin making the movement.' Contrast this with the claim by C. T. Vivian, a stalwart SCLC staff member and, like King, a black Baptist minister, that 'Man, Dr. King was the movement.'

Student Nonviolent Coordinating Committee: A student-led civil rights organization that grew out of the 1960 sit-ins.

The revelation of personal fallibilities have challenged King's saint-like image in early historical works and in the popular imagination. In 1989, Ralph D. Abernathy, King's closest friend and confidant, revealed in his autobiography a number of salacious details about King's alleged affairs. In 1990, Clayborne Carson, director of the King Papers Project at Stanford University, broke the news that King had plagiarised significant portions of his PhD thesis while at Boston University. Much controversy and debate has raged on these subjects since.

Yet at the same time, King's sanctification as an American hero has continued. Since 1986, every third Monday in January has been celebrated as a federal Martin Luther King, Jr. Day holiday. In 2011, the Martin Luther King, Jr. National Memorial was unveiled on the National Mall in Washington DC. King is the first and, to date, only black American to have been honoured by a national holiday and a national monument. Hundreds of streets in the United States have been named, or renamed, after him.

The central focus of this book is not to cast King as a saint or a sinner, nor as a simplified national hero, but, by using the available historical evidence, to fully assess his role and influence as a historical figure. In utilizing the 'Montgomery to Memphis' narrative, it does not look to simply repeat earlier versions of it, but, rather, to rethink and recast it within the light of recent historical scholarship. This study differs from other, particularly shorter, studies of King, in that it locates him firmly within the context of other leaders and organizations, voices and opinions, and tactics and ideologies, which made up the movement as a whole.

There were, this book argues, four distinct stages to King's development as a civil rights leader. The first stage was King's rise to leadership during the 1955–1956 Montgomery bus boycott. During the boycott, King used his status as a black southern Baptist minister to help mobilize the black community. He harnessed the black church both as a spiritual base for legitimizing and shaping the nature of the protest movement, and as a physical base for mass meetings and information dissemination.

The second stage of King's career, stretching from the Montgomery bus boycott to the 1963 Birmingham Campaign, saw King struggling to translate the mass black community activism of the Montgomery bus boycott and the idea of non-violence into a coherent strategy for social and political change. To that end, King, along with other movement activists, helped to found the SCLC. However, early efforts to expand mass black activism through bus boycotts and voter registration campaigns met with little success. Events elsewhere, unfolding largely independently of King and the SCLC, fared much better.

The 1960 student **sit-in** movement led to the formation of a new student-oriented organization in SNCC and forced concessions for the desegregation of public and private facilities in a number of communities. The 1961 **Freedom Rides** were instigated by the **Congress of Racial Equality (CORE)** and forced federal intervention to uphold civil rights in interstate transportation facilities. The sit-ins and the Freedom Rides led the way in demonstrating how non-violent direct action might effectively be applied to bring about social change.

King tried to capitalize on these developments in 1961–1963 in two community-based campaigns in Albany, Georgia, and Birmingham, Alabama. Although King and the SCLC's campaign in Albany at the end of 1961 and the beginning of 1962 encountered a number of difficulties, it proved a vital learning experience in running a far more successful campaign in Birmingham in 1963.

In Birmingham, King and the SCLC developed a strategy of short-term black community mobilization in non-violent direct action demonstrations that successfully forced concessions from whites for civil rights at a local level and engaged support and action from federal government for civil rights at a national level. Historian David J. Garrow notes that the Birmingham strategy marked a significant break from King's earlier attempts to use 'non-violent persuasion', relying on the moral aspects of non-violence to persuade whites to instigate racial change, to a use of 'non-violent coercion' to force change through non-violent direct action demonstrations.

The third stage of King's career, and his most successful, unfolded between the 1963 Birmingham Campaign and the 1965–1966 Chicago, Illinois, Campaign. During this time, King and the SCLC attempted to repeat the strategy of the 1963 Birmingham Campaign in other communities.

Of these campaigns, King and the SCLC's Selma Campaign was by far the most successful, engaging the highest level of public attention, of northern white support, and of federal intervention and action. Following on from the **Civil Rights Act of 1964** which had legislated an end to **segregation** in public facilities and accommodations, President Lyndon B. Johnson introduced and oversaw the passage of the **1965 Voting Rights Act**, which removed obstacles to black voting rights and provided active federal assistance to black voters.

Sit-In: An act designed to directly challenge segregation laws and to force businesses to consider the economic viability of practising segregation.

Freedom Rides: Testing of desegregated bus terminals initiated by CORE in 1961.

Congress of Racial Equality: One of the 'Big Six' civil rights organizations, founded in 1942 and a pioneer in non-violent direct action.

Civil Rights Act of 1964: Required the desegregation of public facilities and accommodations and a range of other pro-civil rights measures.

Segregation: The enforced separation (sometimes legally mandated, sometimes not) of facilities and resources by race.

Voting Rights Act of 1965: Act outlawing discriminatory voting practices such as literacy tests and establishing federal oversight of administering elections.

The fourth stage of King's career is the most complex and generally the least understood. It began with the 1965–1966 Chicago Campaign and ended with King's assassination in Memphis in 1968. During this period, King was forced to re-evaluate the Birmingham strategy in the face of a rapidly changing struggle for black freedom and equality.

With the goal of legislation to compel desegregation and to enforce the black franchise achieved, King and the civil rights movement looked to consolidate these victories while seeking to address new challenges. A number of urban riots in black ghettos of the West and North of the United States between 1965 and 1967 highlighted the problems faced by blacks outside of the South, where King and the SCLC had been predominantly based.

Black Power: Slogan popularized by Stokely Carmichael in 1966 and often associated with black militancy, black nationalism and black armed self-defence.

The popularization of the '**Black Power**' slogan emerged from the experiences of SNCC workers in the rural counties of Alabama and Mississippi, areas where King and the SCLC's influence was also slight, since the Birmingham strategy was focused more on towns and cities. Amid these changes, the **Vietnam War** increasingly overtook civil rights as the most important domestic issue in the United States and the anti-war movement began to sap civil rights movement activists and volunteers.

Vietnam War: A war between the communist North Vietnam and the South Vietnamese regime which the US backed with political and military support from 1955 until its collapse in 1975.

The urban riots, the rise of Black Power, and the anti-war demonstrations, all played their part in prompting a white conservative political backlash to the perceived excesses of liberalism, which conservatives believed was the cause of these developments. King, the SCLC, and the civil rights movement as a whole, were challenged to move beyond desegregation and black enfranchisement to tackle the fundamental economic problems that underpinned black powerlessness and to engage with larger unfolding social and political developments.

King responded to these developments in a number of ways. He tried to tackle the problems faced by urban blacks by implementing the Birmingham strategy of non-violent direct action demonstrations in Chicago. He sought to temper Black Power's anti-white rhetoric and advocacy of black nationalism, black separatism, and black armed self-defence, by insisting that integration and non-violence were still relevant to the struggle for civil rights. He joined the anti-war movement to oppose the United States' actions in Vietnam and he attempted to fuse the energies of the anti-war movement and the civil rights movement in a coalition against incipient white political conservatism.

Poor People's Campaign: Martin Luther King, Jr.'s last campaign that focused on addressing issues of economic injustice.

King further looked to broaden the base of the civil rights movement by forming a coalition of blacks, ethnic minority groups, and poor whites, in a **Poor People's Campaign (PPC)** to take the Birmingham strategy to a new level of mass civil disobedience by staging demonstrations for economic justice in Washington DC. Before he could lead the PPC, however, King was assassinated while supporting a strike by sanitation workers in Memphis in April 1968.

Thus, at the time of his death, King was beginning the next stage of his career, moving beyond a regional civil rights base to a vision of national, and indeed even international, human rights. He was also engaged in developing a fundamentally new strategy of non-violence and civil disobedience in the pursuit of social, political and economic power, an agenda cut tragically short by his assassination, and one that he would never get the chance to implement.

1

The Origins of the Civil Rights Movement

Reconstruction: Period in US history from 1865 to 1877 following the American Civil War when Republicans tried to construct a biracial democracy in the South.

Redemption: Description by southerners of the period following Reconstruction when whites began to seize power and undermine the rights of freedmen.

Separate but Equal: The legal doctrine established in *Plessy* that said facilities for the races could be provided separately if they were of equal standard.

***Plessy v. Ferguson* (1896):** Landmark US Supreme Court decision that established the legal doctrine of 'separate but equal' and led to the expansion of segregation in southern states.

The civil rights movement of the 1950s and 1960s was a distinct phase in a much longer and ongoing black struggle for freedom and equality. Many of the movement's central goals in the 1950s and 1960s related to three constitutional amendments passed almost one hundred years earlier. The **Reconstruction** or Civil Rights Amendments were an attempt to guarantee basic civil rights to former slaves who had previously been viewed as property rather than people. The Thirteenth Amendment, adopted in 1865, abolished slavery [**Doc. 1, p. 136**]. The Fourteenth Amendment, adopted in 1868, promised freedmen 'equal protection under the law' [**Doc. 2, p. 136**]. The Fifteenth Amendment, adopted in 1870, promised that former slaves would not be denied the vote 'on account of race, color, or previous condition of servitude' [**Doc. 3, p. 136**].

After Reconstruction ended in 1877, a period of so-called **Redemption** followed in which southern states undermined blacks' constitutional rights. In the 1890s, segregation became entrenched by a nexus of local and state laws that permeated every aspect of life. In 1896, Louisianan Homer Plessy challenged a state law that required blacks to use separate railway carriages. The US Supreme Court refuted Plessy's claim that he was being denied 'equal protection under the law' as required by the Fourteenth Amendment and countered with the legal doctrine of '**Separate but Equal**'. That doctrine insisted that so long as facilities furnished for the races were of 'equal' standard they could be provided 'separately'. In practice, segregated facilities were often far from equal. However, the ***Plessy v. Ferguson*** decision nourished, grew and sustained segregation over the next 58 years.

The 1890s also saw widespread black disfranchisement. Poll taxes required the payment of a nominal sum to vote. But for former slaves (as well as for some poor whites) this could still be prohibitive. Literacy tests required reading skills to vote. Again, for former slaves with little to no education (and, again, for some poor whites too) this formed an effective obstacle to voting. The fact that biased white election officials administered poll taxes and literacy tests bolstered their effectiveness. Nevertheless, in **Williams v. Mississippi (1898)** the US Supreme Court upheld the use of poll taxes and literacy tests. Other forms of disfranchisement also existed, such as the notorious 'grandfather clause', which stated that if a voter's grandfather was a slave, they were not allowed to vote. For a generation just out of slavery, this disfranchised most black voters. The use of a grandfather clause was eventually outlawed in *Guinn* v. *US* (1915).

Williams v. Mississippi (1898): Landmark US Supreme Court decision that permitted the use of devices such as poll taxes and literacy tests that led to black disfranchisement.

All of these schemes, along with the many others that were employed, sought to circumvent the Fifteenth Amendment without directly defying it. The Fifteenth Amendment, southern states noted, did not prevent denial of the vote through the payment of a poll tax, a literacy test or a grandfather clause. It merely prevented disfranchisement on the grounds of 'race, color, or previous condition of servitude'. By finding ways to disfranchise black voters without explicitly mentioning race as a factor, southern states evaded both the letter and the spirit of the law.

Adding to black powerlessness in southern society was something that Reconstruction had completely failed to address: the lack of black land ownership. One thing former slaves did know how to do was to farm the land. After the Civil War they had hoped to acquire land as a way of becoming truly independent of white landowners. However, Reconstruction had stopped short of redistributing land to freedmen. This left a southern conundrum: whites still had land, but blacks, who were no longer slaves, held the necessary labour to make that land profitable.

White landowners addressed that problem by parcelling out land to black families and developing a system of **sharecropping** and tenant farming. Under that system, black families were leased land in exchange for a portion of their final crop to pay off the rent. Of course, when the time came to settle at the end of the harvest, the white landlord would inform tenants that their crop share was not quite enough to pay off the debt. Year-on-year this debt grew and black families remained in an easily exploited situation. Some states passed laws that prevented black families from moving while they still owed money, which left them in debt peonage.

Sharecropping: An exploitative system of labour that often kept black farmers in debt to white landowners.

Though a semblance of legality surrounded black social, political and economic exploitation in the South, an ever-present threat of violence fundamentally underpinned it. From white terror groups like the **Ku Klux Klan** to elected officials (and sometimes there was no distinction between the two), a conspiracy of fear reigned in the South. Blacks who tried to vote or defy segregation laws, or even breached informal racial etiquette, like failing to move out of the way for a white person in the street or simply looking at them in the wrong kind of way, could face arbitrary consequences ranging

Ku Klux Klan: White vigilante terror group formed at the end of the American Civil War.

Lynching: Extra-legal murder by two or more people of someone suspected of committing a crime.

Nightriding: White vigilantism against and intimidation of black farmers.

Whitecapping: Extra-legal enforcement of community values by secret societies that was often directed against blacks.

from a reprimand to a beating, or death. Over 3,000 recorded **lynchings** occurred in the South between 1882 and 1922. **Nightriding** and **whitecapping** in rural areas kept black farmers in check.

New black leaders emerged to tackle the new problems in an age of segregation, disenfranchisement, white economic exploitation and white violence. Foremost among these was Booker T. Washington. Washington was born into slavery and went on to become the first leader of Tuskegee Normal and Industrial Institute, which became an enduring and successful symbol of black education. It still exists today as Tuskegee University.

In his 1895 Atlanta Address, Washington laid out his philosophy that blacks should 'concentrate all their energies on industrial education, and accumulation of wealth, and the conciliation of the South'. That is, he advocated the uplifting of the race through education, hard work and cooperation with whites. He preached that through doing this blacks could earn their rightful place in American society.

Washington's philosophy has led to him being labelled an 'accommodationist', that is, someone who kowtowed to white authority. More recent evaluations by historians have demonstrated that Washington, while espousing conciliatory rhetoric, at the same time contributed funds to legal battles against segregation and disfranchisement.

Born and reared a southerner, Washington knew the value of cultivating wealthy and influential whites and he was wary of alienating them. He argued that taking too forthright a stand against white discrimination could lead to damaging and deadly retribution. Like many black southerners, Washington was forced to wear two faces, one for dealing with influential whites and one for dealing with blacks. It was a survival strategy that was drummed into many black children by their parents over the years.

When Washington died in 1915, one of his chief rivals during his lifetime, W. E. B. Du Bois, emerged as the leading spokesperson of black America. Born in the North, Du Bois was the first black to receive a doctorate from Harvard and he was a founder member of the Niagara Movement, a forerunner of America's oldest civil rights organization, the **National Association for the Advancement of Colored People (NAACP)**, founded in 1909.

National Association for the Advancement of Colored People: Founded in 1909 in New York, the NAACP is America's oldest civil rights organization and played a crucial role in laying the legal foundations for the civil rights movement in the 1940s and 1950s.

In opposition to Washington's perceived 'accomodationism', Du Bois advocated 'protest', stating that 'we must unceasingly and firmly oppose' racial discrimination. Du Bois became editor of the NAACP newspaper *The Crisis*, where he continued to advocate an unrelenting black struggle against white supremacy. Some have noted that as a northerner Du Bois was able to be less restrained than Washington since he was more distanced from the day-to-day realities of black oppression in the South.

Other leaders, such as Marcus Garvey, advocated black 'separatism' and 'nationalism'. Garvey, who was a Jamaican, through the **Universal Negro**

Improvement Association (UNIA) helped to build one of the earliest black mass movements in the United States during the 1920s. Garvey advocated black pride and the building of a black ancestral home in Africa. His separatist 'Back-to-Africa' rhetoric stood in contrast to Washington's call for accommodation and Du Bois's call for protest.

In fact, the Back-to-Africa and black nationalist ideals built on earlier legacies in the United States in movements led by figures such as Henry McNeal Turner and Martin Delaney. Future **Nation of Islam** spokesperson Malcolm X's father was a Garveyite and Garvey's ideas influenced Malcolm's later expressions of black pride.

Though the schema of 'accommodation,' 'protest' and 'separatism' has often been used to typify black responses to the age of segregation, the more historians have examined the origins of the civil rights movement, the richer, more complex and more diverse the various strands and influences of black responses have appeared.

Although much focus has been placed on male leaders and male-dominated organizations, women played important roles too. Ida B. Wells, an African American Memphis journalist, reported and helped to raise awareness of the horrors of lynching to a national audience. Many black women ran and formed the vital backbones of local branches of male-dominated national organizations. The **National Council of Negro Women (NCNW)**, founded by Mary McLeod Bethune in 1935, sought to harness and coordinate women's leadership contributions.

White women, such as Jesse Daniel Ames, worked for racial change through organizations like the **Commission on Interracial Cooperation (CIC)**, founded in 1918. In 1930, Ames founded the **Association of Southern Women for the Prevention of Lynching (ASWPL)**.

The multiplicity of individuals and organizations that paved the way for the emergence of the civil rights movement is too extensive to fully name and list here, but each has its own story to tell about the movement's influences.

Take for example the four of the '**Big Six**' civil rights organizations that were founded before the 1950s (the other two, the Southern Christian Leadership Conference and the Student Nonviolent Coordinating Committee were founded in 1957 and 1960). The NAACP used lobbying and later litigation to pave the way for black advancement in Congress and in the courts. The **National Urban League (NUL)**, founded in 1910, looked to address the social welfare and employment conditions of blacks in cities. The **Brotherhood of Sleeping Car Porters Union (BSCPU)**, founded in 1925, speaks to the importance of unions and labour organizing in the origins of the movement. The Congress of Racial Equality (CORE), founded in 1942, had radical religious pacifist roots and was a pioneer of non-violent direct action.

Universal Negro Improvement Association: Founded by Jamaican Marcus Garvey in 1914, the black nationalist UNIA led the United States' earliest mass black movement in the 1920s.

Back-to-Africa: The idea that blacks are best served leaving the US and going back to Africa.

Nation of Islam: Founded in 1930 in Detroit, the NOI is one of the most prominent Black Muslim groups in the United States.

National Council of Negro Women: Black women's advocacy group founded by Mary McLeod Bethune in 1935.

Commission on Interracial Cooperation: Formed in Atlanta in 1918 to help address southern racial problems and a forerunner of the Southern Regional Council.

Association of Southern Women for the Prevention of Lynching: Founded by Jesse Daniel Ames in 1930 to petition, lobby and fundraise to prevent lynching.

Big Six: The term used by the press to refer to the leaders of the 'Big Six' civil rights organizations: BSPCU, CORE, NAACP, NUL, SCLC and SNCC.

National Urban League: Founded in 1910 in New York, the NUL focuses on providing social services and enhancing the economic conditions of urban blacks in America's largest cities.

Brotherhood of Sleeping Car Porters Union: Labour union formed in 1925 to defend the interests of its predominantly black membership.

If individuals and organizations helped to form the framework for the movement, black community institutions laid its foundations. Black community-building was, ironically, aided by a segregated order that necessitated the creation of a small but influential black middle class in most southern towns and cities.

Black teachers were the largest representatives in this group, staffing segregated black schools. Although most black schools were severely underfunded by states in comparison to white schools, they did offer a place where black children encountered successful black authority figures and where they could be educated about the history of and their responsibilities to the race. Black ministers were the next largest group in the black middle class and played an important role in stewarding churches that were a place for black worship and fellowship as well as a meeting place for numerous other black community activities.

The small black middle class was made up of sundry other constituencies. Black journalists and the black media (in print and later over the radio waves) helped disseminate both national and community news and often served as a mouthpiece and information centre for black activism. Black businessmen brought jobs and wealth to the black community (albeit on a limited basis) and financed and led black community initiatives for advancement and protest.

The civil rights movement sprang from and went into the unlikeliest of places, from black-owned barber shops and beauticians to black fraternities and funeral parlours (someone had to prepare and bury the black dead for interment in segregated cemeteries), and black juke joints and doctor's offices. With limited resources, the movement needed to draw on every pre-existing building block for community organizing that it could.

The movement was also profoundly shaped by larger historical events.

Great Migration: The population shift of blacks from the rural South to the urban North and West over the course of the twentieth century.

The **Great Migration** of blacks from the South to the cities of the North, Midwest and West of the United States over the course of the twentieth century, estimated at around 6 million people from 1910 to 1970, impacted in a variety of ways.

Blacks moving North escaped southern segregation and disfranchisement, although many soon discovered that they had merely switched distinctly rural problems for distinctly urban ones, like ghetto housing, employment discrimination, and competition for space and facilities with whites and other ethnic groups. Nevertheless, the black vote that expanded in these cities became increasingly influential. In 1948, black votes made the difference in the election of Democratic President Harry S. Truman. As black political strength grew, so too did black political influence nationally and locally, and white politicians had to be more responsive to the needs of the black community. The journey North and West nationalized the black struggle beyond the South. Meanwhile, family and community members that shuttled between North and South and stayed in close contact with those at home created new support and information networks.

World War I and the industrial jobs it created in the North acted as a catalyst for black migration. Black leaders like W. E. B. Du Bois advocated 'closing ranks' for the war and proving the worth of black labour and black soldiers to the United States in hope of a just reward afterwards. Blacks played a significant role in America's wartime economy and in the war effort, although they were relegated mainly to menial jobs in service. When allowed to serve in combat roles they did so only on a strictly segregated basis.

On return from the war, the expected thanks and reward were not forth-coming. Instead, a Red Summer of racial violence raged in 1919 as returning black and white soldiers competed for jobs, and whites sought to put blacks that had served in the US uniform 'back in their place'. Having faithfully served their country, blacks were far more inclined to resist this backward step. Race riots broke out in over 35 cities. In Chicago, a black youth who inadvertently swam into an ethnically white area was stoned by whites and drowned. The thirteen days of rioting that followed ended in 38 deaths (23 blacks, 15 whites) and 537 casualties. In rural Elaine, Arkansas, attempts to form a black sharecroppers' union ended in a race riot in which possibly hundreds of black men, women and children were killed by local whites.

The 1920s continued a period of cultural ferment and racial and ethnic tension. The resurgence of the second Ku Klux Klan, relaunched in 1915, showed that if the Great Migration had nationalized the black struggle for civil rights, then white resistance to it had national dimensions too. The Klan enjoyed its most successful political fortunes in the 1920s, moving from rural areas into the cities, and from the South into the rest of the United States. Membership grew to a peak of 6 million. Detroit recruited 40,000 members to the city's Klan. The Klan also recruited significant numbers on the West Coast from California to Oregon. Klansmen won a number of political offices including the governorships of Colorado and Indiana.

Meanwhile, Harlem, New York's black district, saw a flowering of the arts in the 1920s in what became known as the **Harlem Renaissance**. Musicians like Fats Waller, Duke Ellington and Jelly Roll Morton popularized jazz music; writers like poet Langston Hughes, novelist Zora Neal Hurston and playwright Jean Toomer drew on the black experience for their material and black intellectuals like Alain Locke, the first black American to attend Oxford University in the United Kingdom as a Rhodes scholar, proclaimed the birth of a 'New Negro'. The Harlem Renaissance showcased black musicians, com-posers, writers, artists and actors; it drew on the black American experience and gave it mainstream cultural standing, and it gave lie to the stereotype of black Americans as simple, uneducated, backwoods rural folk.

Harlem Renaissance: A flowering of black arts and culture in Harlem, New York, in the 1920s.

New Deal: The collective name for a number of programmes and organizations created by the Franklin D. Roosevelt presidential administration to alleviate the effects of the Great Depression in the 1930s.

The Great Depression that began in 1929 and the **New Deal** that followed from 1933 to 1938 gave rise to some fundamental changes in US and southern society. Blacks were hit disproportionally harder by the Depression as competition for jobs with whites increased. President Franklin D. Roosevelt's aim for the New Deal was to bring about economic recovery and not specifically to address civil rights, although more liberal politicians who were sympathetic to the plight of blacks headed many New Deal agencies. Equally, there were unsympathetic, even overtly racist, heads of New Deal agencies and programmes.

Nevertheless, elements of Roosevelt's New Deal gave blacks hope. Roosevelt's wife Eleanor was a strong and open proponent of civil rights and black equality. The extended reach of federal government that the New Deal promulgated, while at times seemingly ambiguous about or directly opposed to racial change, did offer the promise of a more active national ally against southern states that continued to operate under a blanket policy of racial discrimination.

Emancipation Proclamation: 1863 Executive Order by President Abraham Lincoln that started the process of slave emancipation during the American Civil War.

This support was reflected in voting patterns. The majority of blacks had voted Republican since the Civil War as the party of President Abraham Lincoln and the **Emancipation Proclamation**. But as Republicans eschewed black votes and the national Democratic Party appeared to serve black needs better in the 1930s (the southern wing of the Democratic Party meanwhile remained staunchly conservative and pro-segregation) black voters defected to the Democrats *en masse*.

March on Washington Movement: A 1941 movement designed to place pressure on the federal government to adopt fair employment practices during World War II.

To this day, blacks constitute one of the most dependable block votes for the Democratic Party; it is no coincidence that America's first black president Barack Obama is a Democrat. As more blacks voted Democrat, the party grew more supportive of their cause.

One of the far-reaching consequences of the New Deal was its policy of collectivization and mechanization in agriculture. This displaced black sharecroppers and tenant farmers from the land and more blacks moved into growing southern towns and cities. The urbanization of the southern black population created the larger black communities that were needed to sustain civil rights protests in later decades.

Executive Order 8802: Issued by President Franklin D. Roosevelt, this forbade racial discrimination in wartime industry hiring practices and set up the Fair Employment Practices Committee to enforce the ban.

World War II accelerated the trend of black urbanization by expanding more new job opportunities in industry. It also finally dragged the US economy out of depression. President of the black Brotherhood of Sleeping Car Porters Union, A. Philip Randolph, proposed a **March on Washington Movement** in 1941 that threatened to lead 100,000 blacks on the nation's capital to secure equal wartime employment for black workers. President Roosevelt responded by issuing **Executive Order 8802** to create the **Fair Employment Practices Committee (FEPC)** to monitor racial discrimination in federal hiring practices.

Fair Employment Practices Committee: Created by President Franklin D. Roosevelt's Executive Order 8802 to monitor racial discrimination in federal hiring practices.

Learning from their experience in World War I, blacks explicitly tied their participation in the war effort to civil rights at home. Black newspaper the *Pittsburg Courier* launched a '**Double-V**' campaign for the defeat of Nazism abroad and the defeat of racism at home. The black press and the black public embraced this sentiment.

During World War II, blacks once again served in the armed forces in a segregated US military. This time, they were rewarded in 1948 when President Harry S. Truman issued **Executive Order 9981**, which led to the desegregation of the military. The military remains one of American's most integrated institutions.

In 1946, Truman had established a President's Committee on Civil Rights, which the following year produced the report *To Secure These Rights*, which advocated federal anti-lynching measures and the abolition of poll taxes along with other pro-civil rights legislation. Many of these proposed reforms were subsequently blocked in Congress where southern politicians opposed them. The conflict between different branches of federal government over civil rights presaged the later battles that lay ahead.

Immediately following World War II, the United States became embroiled in a **Cold War** with the Soviet Union. The Cold War had a contradictory impact on the civil rights struggle. On the one hand, it led to a more politically conservative and socially repressive climate in the United States, which found its apotheosis in the anti-communist witch-hunts of Republican Senator Joseph T. McCarthy in the late 1940s and early 1950s. Any perceived left of centre cause risked the accusation of harbouring communist sympathies and opponents of civil rights used McCarthy-ite sentiments and anti-communist rhetoric to curtail the activities of many existing civil rights leaders and organizations.

On the other hand, the Cold War made the United States ever more aware of the contradiction between existing racial discrimination and claims to represent global democracy for all. The Soviet Union responded to criticism about its denial of human rights in Eastern Europe by pointing to the United States' track record in race relations. Anti-colonial struggles by non-whites in Africa, Asia, and the Far East created newly emerging nations where the stance of the two superpowers on the question of race was influential in winning support.

One of the civil rights organizations that did continue to flourish in Cold War America, largely due to its staunch anti-communist stance, was the NAACP. In the mid-1930s NAACP attorney Charles Hamilton Houston mapped out a legal strategy for undermining segregation. This was vigorously pursued and implemented by his protégé and successor, Thurgood Marshall.

In the late 1930s and early 1940s, Marshall won a number of favourable rulings to equalize the salaries of black and white teachers. He went on to

Double-V: Campaign launched by black newspaper the *Pittsburgh Courier* for victory against fascism abroad and racism in the US during World War II.

Executive Order 9981: Issued by President Harry S. Truman, this set in motion the process of desegregating the US armed forces.

Cold War: A war of words and posturing, although rarely outright head-to-head conflict, fought between the US and Soviet Union between *c.* 1947 and 1991.

Morgan v. *Virginia* (1946): US Supreme Court ruling that outlawed segregation on interstate buses.

successfully argue a number of landmark cases before the US Supreme Court. *Smith* v. *Allwright* (1944) outlawed the use of all-white Democratic Party primaries that blocked black access to politics in a number of southern states. **Morgan v. Virginia** (1946) made segregated seating on interstate bus routes illegal. In a series of court cases in higher education, *Missouri ex rel. Gaines* v. *Canada* (1938), *Sipuel* v. *Oklahoma State Regents* (1948), *McLaurin* v. *Oklahoma State Regents* (1950), and *Sweatt* v. *Painter* (1950), Marshall successfully challenged the legality of segregation in higher education and narrowed the available options of university policy in the area.

Brown v. *Board of Education* (1954): Landmark US Supreme Court ruling that outlawed segregation in schools.

A critical legal breakthrough came in **Brown v. Board of Education (1954)**, when the US Supreme Court ruled that segregation in schools was unconstitutional [**Doc. 4, p. 136**]. Reversing its earlier *Plessy* ruling, the court concluded that 'in the field of public education the doctrine of "separate but equal" has no place'. After handing down the *Brown* decision the court delayed its implementation for a year to take advice on how to proceed. Many white southerners opposed *Brown*. Some vowed a campaign of 'massive resistance' and Mississippi led the way in the formation of the first White Citizens' Council dedicated to preventing school desegregation.

The reaction to *Brown* at a national level was not encouraging either. Republican President Dwight D. Eisenhower refused to back the *Brown* decision strongly in public. In private he confided that his recent appointment of Earl Warren as US Supreme Court chief justice was the 'biggest damn fool mistake' he had ever made. In March 1956, 101 southern congressmen signed the '**Southern Manifesto**' in outright opposition to *Brown*. There were even rumours of dissent within the Supreme Court. Some justices who had been persuaded to sign up to a unanimous decision in *Brown* now argued for a lenient implementation order to appease opponents.

Southern Manifesto: Document signed by 101 southern congressmen declaring the *Brown* decision unconstitutional.

Consequently, when the court issued its implementation order in May 1955, it appeared to backtrack. The court set no definite guidelines for when school desegregation should begin, nor did it indicate how it should be carried out. It devolved the details and responsibility for school desegregation to local school boards and to local and state judges. Many of these were white southerners opposed to desegregation. School desegregation, the court informed them, should proceed 'with all deliberate speed'. Many interpreted this as a mandate for indefinite delay.

The NAACP bore the brunt of the white backlash to *Brown*. Many of its southern members were persecuted for their activities and local branch membership figures dwindled as a result. In 1956, Alabama effectively barred the NAACP from operating in the state altogether.

The determination of whites to maintain the racial status quo in the South was powerfully illustrated with the killing of 14-year-old Emmett Till in Money, Mississippi, in 1955. Till, from Chicago, was visiting his uncle when he tried to impress his friends at a local store by flirting with a local white woman. Accounts differ over what Till may have said or done. The transgression of racial etiquette, whatever it was, or perceived to be, cost him his life. That night, the white woman's husband and her brother dragged Till from his uncle's home, murdered him, and dumped his body in the Tallahatchie River. At the funeral back in Chicago, Till's mother insisted on an open casket so the world could see what had happened to her now horribly disfigured son. Graphic images of Till's corpse were carried by a number of black newspapers and magazines. Growing opposition to the *Brown* decision, coupled with Till's murder, which underscored white disregard for the law (Till's killers were swiftly exonerated by an all-white jury), fuelled black anger and drove demands for change.

By the mid-1950s it was clear that another new era in the black struggle for freedom and equality was dawning. The NAACP had won its greatest victory in the courts after decades of litigation. Yet, despite the NAACP having won the legal argument against segregation in schools through the courts, white southerners now insisted that they would still resist any change at any cost. As blacks were only too aware from past experience, winning favourable federal court rulings, legislation, and Constitutional amendments was one thing; enforcing them was quite another.

It was at this delicately poised crossroads in US race relations that the Montgomery bus boycott began in December 1955. In turn, that protest launched a new black leader, Rev. Dr. Martin Luther King, Jr., into the national spotlight.

Further reading

Much has been made recently of placing the civil rights movement of the 1950s and 1960s in the context of a 'long civil rights movement' that preceded and outlasted those two decades. An influential statement of intent in this respect is Jacquelyn Dowd Hall, 'The Long Civil Rights Movement and the Political Uses of the Past', *Journal of American History* 91:4 (March 2005): 1233–1263. For a critique of this perspective see Sundiata Keita Cha-Jua and Clarence Lang, 'The "Long Movement" as Vampire: Temporal and Spatial Fallacies in Recent Black Freedom Studies', *Journal of African American History* 92:2 (Spring 2007): 265–288.

Many books have charted the larger historical forces and developments that shaped the movement. The following provide good starting points: Isabel Wilkerson, *The Warmth of Other Suns: The Epic Story of America's Great Migration* (2010); Lauren Rebecca Skarloff, *Black Culture and the New Deal: The Quest for Civil Rights in the Roosevelt Era* (2009); Maggi Morehouse, *Fighting in the Jim Crow Army: Black Men and Women Remember World War II*

(2000); Mary L. Dudziak, *Cold War Civil Rights: Race and the Image of Democracy* (2000); and Stephen J. Whitfield, *A Death in the Delta: The Story of Emmett Till* (1988). The best sociological study of the origins of the movement in the 1950s is Aldon D. Morris, *Origins of the Civil Rights Movement: Black Communities Organizing for Change* (1984).

The struggle to desegregate schools and universities unfolded at the same time as other civil rights campaigns although those stories are often relegated to the sidelines. So too is the NAACP's influential litigation role in the 1940s and 1950s and the leadership of Thurgood Marshall. On these, see Patricia Sullivan, *Lift Every Voice: The NAACP and the Making of the Civil Rights Movement* (2009) and Mark V. Tushnet, *Making Constitutional Law: Thurgood Marshall and the Supreme Court, 1962–1991* (1997).

Brown v. *Board of Education* was a crucial trigger for movement activism in the 1950s. Its history is charted in Richard Kluger, *Simple Justice: The History of Brown v. Board of Education and Black America's Struggle for Equality* (Latest Edition, 2004) and Michael Klarman, *From Jim Crow to Civil Rights: The Supreme Court and the Struggle for Racial Equality* (2004).

White opposition to *Brown* is surveyed in George Lewis, *Massive Resistance: The White Response to the Civil Rights Movement* (2006). The Little Rock school crisis is covered in Karen Anderson, *Little Rock: Race and Resistance at Central High School* (2009); Tony A. Freyer, *Little Rock on Trial: Cooper v. Aaron and School Desegregation* (2007); and John A. Kirk, *Redefining the Color Line: Black Activism in Little Rock, Arkansas, 1940–1970* (2002).

Part 2

KING AND A FLEDGLING MOVEMENT, 1955–1960

2

Martin Luther King, Jr.'s Early Life, 1929–1955

Martin Luther King, Jr. was born in Atlanta, Georgia, on 15 January 1929. From the beginning, his life was steeped in the traditions of the black southern Baptist church. 'Religion for me is life,' King wrote in one of his college essays [**Doc. 5, p. 138**]. King's mother, Alberta Williams King, was the only daughter of successful Atlanta minister Adam Daniel (A. D.) Williams, the son of a black slave preacher. King's father, Martin Luther King, Sr., known affectionately to family and friends as 'Daddy' King, was raised in rural Georgia and was the son of a farmer. An ambitious man, at the age of 18 Daddy King set off for Atlanta determined to better himself through education. After graduating from Morehouse College he married into the influential Williams family and later inherited his father-in-law's pulpit at Ebenezer Baptist Church on downtown Auburn Avenue.

King spent his early years living with his parents, his older sister Christine King, his younger brother Alfred Daniel Williams King (A. D.) and his maternal grandparents, at 501 Auburn Avenue, located just a short distance from Ebenezer. King's familial involvement with the church placed him at the heart of black community life. As one of the few institutions wholly funded by blacks, the church provided a hub of black religious, social and cultural life, and offered a degree of shelter and independence from whites.

Reflecting the historically prominent status of the church in the black community, the job of a black minister conferred considerable social standing and authority. In the South at the time, most black men were employed in menial and low paid jobs, while many black women worked in white homes as domestics to supplement family income. The ministry was one of the few occupations for blacks that enjoyed economic independence from whites since the church congregation funded the position. Daddy King's standing in the black community, together with his financial frugality, ensured a relatively comfortable existence for the King family. 'It is quite easy for me to think of the universe as basically friendly mainly because of my uplifting hereditary and environmental circumstances,' M. L. King, Jr. later reflected.

Yet although King's upbringing ensured that he was relatively isolated from the harsher aspects of southern racism, it was impossible to hide completely from that wider social reality. Indeed, some of King's most vivid recollections of childhood involved instances of racial discrimination.

As a child, like many other black southerners, King counted white children among his playmates. However, when it was time to start school, the veil of segregation began to fall on those friendships. When they enrolled at their respective segregated schools in Atlanta at the age of six, King's best white friend informed him that 'his father had demanded that he would play with me no more'. This ended their friendship.

At the age of 14, King travelled to Dublin, Georgia, where he participated in a school oratorical contest, speaking on the subject of 'The Negro and the Constitution'. On the way back, he and his teacher were forced to surrender their coach seats to white passengers and to stand for 90 miles until they reached Atlanta. 'It was', King recalled, 'the angriest I have ever been in my life.' Such episodes made King wonder 'how could I love a race of people [who] hated me' and how he could reconcile that feeling with the demands of Christianity to love all people.

After graduation from high school in 1944 at the age of 15, King followed in his father's and his maternal grandfather's footsteps by enrolling at Atlanta's Morehouse College. King entered Morehouse at such a young age because, in the words of college president Benjamin E. Mays, a respected scholar of black religion, 'The Second World War was playing havoc with the College, for our students were being drafted in large numbers. In this crisis, we decided to take into the freshman class students who had only finished the eleventh grade.'

Given the King family's church tradition, there was great expectation that King would enter the ministry. However, King initially contemplated becoming a doctor or a lawyer while opting to major in sociology at Morehouse. Immersed in the black church from birth, King felt that he had simply wandered into religion rather than actively accepting it into his life. He had joined the Ebenezer congregation at the age of five, 'not out of any dynamic conviction, but out of a childhood desire to keep up with my sister'. Even when he was baptized, King later admitted, he simply went through the motions of the ceremony without comprehending its full significance. Thus, by the age of 13, King was already beginning to question fundamental Christian orthodoxy, shocking 'my Sunday school class by denying the bodily resurrection of Jesus. Doubts began to spring forth unrelentingly.'

King's reservations about the southern black Baptist church continued to grow. He disapproved of the way that many black preachers used raw emotionalism by employing the whooping and hollering of the black folk pulpit to engage their congregations. King preferred a more cerebral approach by using intellectual arguments to get his message from pulpit to pew. He was also concerned at the way many black preachers sermonized about the promise of a better life in the next world instead of tackling the more immediate day-to-day problems that blacks faced under segregation.

Nevertheless, King's continuing studies of the Bible at Morehouse convinced him that, despite his ongoing vocational doubts, Scripture contained 'many profound truths which one could not escape'. Moreover, academic clerics at Morehouse demonstrated to King that a ministerial career could be successfully combined with intellectual rigour. To Daddy King's delight, his son finally decided to enter the ministry, serving as assistant pastor at Ebenezer while continuing his studies at Morehouse. In February 1948, Daddy King presided at his son's ordination as a Baptist minister.

As a young entrant into college, King struggled to make good grades at Morehouse. But his experiences there influenced more than just his academic development. While at Morehouse, King became a member of the NAACP. He also participated in an interracial Intercollegiate Council with other Atlanta schools and colleges. King's attitude toward whites softened somewhat and he became convinced that a new generation of white southerners might offer hope for more enlightened race relations in the future.

While in college, King also got his first taste of life outside of the South on summer trips to earn money by picking tobacco in Connecticut. Although the young King idealized just how free life for blacks in the North was – racial discrimination did exist there, albeit not in the same legally mandated form as in the South – the escape from southern segregation was a revelation to him. King found that he could enjoy more personal freedom in the North than he ever could in Atlanta. Changing trains in Washington DC for a segregated journey back home to the South, King felt the curtain 'dropped on my selfhood' yet again.

The desire to escape the South was one factor in King's decision to study at Crozer Theological Seminary in Chester, Pennsylvania, after graduating from Morehouse. The move also fulfilled King's desire to gain greater independence from his father. Moreover, the small, liberal and predominantly white Crozer came highly recommended by King's professors at Morehouse because of its nationally known reputation.

This time a longer stay in the North opened King's eyes to racial attitudes there. One day, he and a friend went into nearby Philadelphia for food. They sat ignored for 30 minutes before finally demanding service. When the food came there was sand deliberately scattered in the vegetables. On another occasion, while King and his friends were on a double date in New Jersey, a restaurant proprietor chased them out of the establishment with a gun after refusing them service.

While at Crozer, King became romantically involved with a white woman and even considered a proposal of marriage. Friends intervened, warning of how difficult life would be for an interracial couple and how it would make a return to the South impossible. In most southern states at the time, interracial marriages were banned by law. Painful though it was, the two agreed to end their six-month relationship. King learned from these episodes how profoundly race shaped social attitudes and conduct in the North as well as the South.

King's academic performance at Crozer was much better than at Morehouse. His maturing attitude to study earned him the status of class valedictorian when he graduated in 1951. Studies at Crozer exposed King to a number of ideas that he eagerly explored, from economic historian Karl Marx's critique of capitalism to theologian Walter Rauschenbush's writings about the **Social Gospel**, to lectures on pacifism and Gandhian non-violence.

Social Gospel: A movement and philosophy that applies Christian ethics to social problems.

Throughout his studies, King took a stance of healthy scepticism in all of his encounters with new theories and philosophies. Notably, he developed a fondness for philosopher G. W. Hegel's dialectic method of analysis. This involved taking two opposing sides of an argument, weighing both positive and negative points in each, and finding an answer by using a synthesis of elements in both. This dialectical method of reasoning, which sought compromise and reconciliation between different points of view, would remain central to King's approach to problem-solving throughout his life.

After graduating from Crozer, King applied to several schools to study for a PhD before finally deciding to enrol in the philosophy faculty at Boston University. King chose Boston at the recommendation of his Crozer professors and because he was keen to study under Dr Edgar S. Brightman whose ideas on '**personalism**' had aroused King's interest. Personalism insisted that human personality, which all individuals possessed, was the ultimate value in the world. This reaffirmed King's belief in the essential worth of all human beings. Applied to his developing ideas about religion and race, this meant that segregation, which denied the equal humanity of black and white citizens, was fundamentally evil and at odds with God's will. After Brightman's death at the end of King's first year of study, King transferred his registration to Brightman's protégé L. Harold DeWolf in the theology faculty. Further broadening his knowledge of philosophy at Boston, King took classes at nearby Harvard University.

Personalism: A theological and philosophical belief in the importance and worth of an individual's actions.

While studying at Boston, through a mutual friend King met his future wife Coretta Scott. Scott, from rural Alabama, was studying on a scholarship at Boston's New England Conservatory of Music with aspirations to become a classical singer. Initially, Daddy King opposed his son's plans to marry Coretta since he preferred a match that would see Martin, Jr. marry into a family in Atlanta's black elite. At his first meeting with Coretta, Daddy King 'went a little too far, mentioning names, women to whom M. L. had proposed marriage' in his eagerness to dissuade her. King took his father to one side and told him, 'I must marry Coretta. She's the most important thing to come into my life . . . I know you don't really approve, but this is what I have to do.' King's father eventually relented. On 18 June 1953, Daddy King married the couple at the Scott family home in rural Alabama and soon after baptized his new daughter-in-law at Ebenezer.

As King's residential studies at Boston came to a close he began the search for a pastorate where he could work while writing up his PhD dissertation. Daddy King was keen for his son to return to Atlanta as co-pastor of Ebenezer and persuaded Benjamin Mays to offer his son a faculty position at Morehouse to combine with his church duties. Although King did want to preach in a southern city, he still yearned for independence from his father. He therefore rejected the idea of returning to Atlanta and arranged to deliver a trial sermon for a position at First Baptist Church in Chattanooga, Tennessee.

At the same time, through a family friend, King learned of a vacant position at Dexter Avenue Baptist Church in Montgomery. Dexter had recently fired its controversial and outspoken pastor Vernon Johns, a reflection of the notoriously tough treatment that the church handed out to its ministers. Unperturbed, King arranged a trial sermon there, which was well received. In April 1954, King accepted Dexter's offer of the post and took up his new job the following September.

King quickly set about putting his stamp on his new role. He made it quite clear that he would oversee major decisions affecting the church. King firmly informed the Dexter church board members that 'leadership never ascends from the pew to the pulpit, but invariably descends from the pulpit to the pew'.

Although such an assertion might at first glance seem arrogant, King understood and fully accepted that taking on such authority also meant accepting a burden of responsibility. In return for being given the reins of leadership, King offered total commitment and devotion to duty. In his leadership of the church, as with his later leadership of the civil rights movement, he was both conscientious and dutiful. For King, leadership constituted both a blessing and a curse. As he revealingly told his congregation on one occasion, 'The honors and privileges that often come as a result of leadership contribute only one side of the picture. The greater the privileges, the greater the responsibilities and sacrifices.'

King proceeded to set up a host of new church committees, including a social and political action committee. He linked church-based activities to the wider community by joining the local Montgomery branch of the NAACP.

Alabama Council on Human Relations: Interracial organization affiliated with the Southern Regional Council.

King also attended meetings of the Montgomery branch of the **Alabama Council on Human Relations (ACHR)**, a state affiliate of the white liberal organization the **Southern Regional Council (SRC)**, which was headquartered in Atlanta. The ACHR was the only interracial organization prepared to address the question of racial change in Montgomery at the time. King went about proving himself worthy of his new church position by investing a great deal of time preparing polished sermons that pleased his new congregation with their performance from the pulpit on Sunday mornings.

Southern Regional Council: Atlanta-based interracial civil rights organization founded in 1944.

King finally completed his PhD thesis while working at Dexter and was awarded his doctorate from Boston in June 1955. On 17 November 1955, the Kings' first child, Yolanda Denise King, was born. King's early life had taken him to where he wanted to be: an educated preacher in an affluent southern church with a comfortable family life. But history was about to intervene and change the course of his life forever.

Further reading

The best substantial biographies of King all came out in the mid-1980s. Adam Fairclough, *To Redeem the Soul of America: The Southern Christian Leadership Conference and Martin Luther King, Jr.* (1987) provides a good analytical overview; David J. Garrow, *Bearing the Cross: Martin Luther King, Jr. and the Southern Christian Leadership Conference* (1986) provides narrative detail; and the Taylor Branch trilogy, *Parting the Waters: America in the King Years, 1954–63* (1988), *Pillar of Fire: America in the King Years, 1963–65* (1998) and *At Canaan's Edge: America in the King Years, 1965–68* (2006), is exhaustive. First-hand accounts from King's family circle include: Martin Luther King, Sr., with Clayton Riley, *Daddy King: An Autobiography* (1980); Christine Farris King, *My Brother Martin: A Sister Remembers Growing Up with Rev. Dr. Martin Luther King, Jr.* (2003); Coretta Scott King, *My Life With Martin Luther King, Jr.* (1969); and Dexter Scott King, *Growing Up King: An Intimate Memoir* (2003).

3

The Montgomery Bus Boycott, 1955–1956

On the late afternoon of 1 December 1955, 42-year-old Rosa L. Parks, a seamstress in a downtown Montgomery, Alabama, department store boarded her bus home from work. As the bus moved along its route it began to fill with people. White bus driver J. Fred Blake told Parks and other black passengers sitting next to and across the row from her to 'let me have those front seats'.

In the system of racial segregation that existed in Montgomery at the time, the ten seats at the front of the bus were reserved for white passengers and the ten seats at the back of the bus were reserved for black passengers. In the middle section, whites filled the seats from the front, and blacks filled the seats from the back, on a first come, first served, basis. On that particular evening, blacks occupied all of the seats in the middle section. Parks was sitting in the row next to the white section. The white section was crowded with standing passengers but there was space for blacks to stand at the back.

Asked again, Parks still refused to budge. 'Well, if you don't stand up, I'm going to call the police and have you arrested,' Blake told her. 'You may do that,' Parks replied. Blake then went to inform the police. A few minutes later, a squad car arrived, and two policemen boarded the bus. 'Why don't you stand up?' asked one of the officers. 'Why do you push us around?' Parks demanded. 'I do not know, but the law is the law and you are under arrest,' the officer replied. The policemen then hauled Parks off to the police station where she was charged with breaking Montgomery's city bus segregation ordinance.

News of Parks's arrest quickly reached one of Montgomery's leading black activists, Edgar Daniel (E. D.) Nixon. A railroad porter, Nixon was head of the black Brotherhood of Sleeping Car Porters (BSCPU) union in Alabama, and president of the Progressive Democratic Association, the political voice of black Democratic Party supporters in Alabama. As a former president of the

Montgomery NAACP, Nixon had known Parks for a number of years as she had served as his branch secretary. When Nixon called the Montgomery police station to find out exactly what had happened, he was curtly told by a police officer that it was 'None of your so-and-so business.'

Nixon then attempted to contact black attorney Fred D. Gray. The young, recently qualified attorney was, alongside Charles D. Langford, one of only two black attorneys practising in Montgomery at the time, and the only one willing to accept civil rights cases. When Nixon discovered that Gray was out of town on business, he contacted white attorney Clifford Durr. Clifford and his wife Virginia Durr belonged to a small section of the Montgomery white community – a section found in white communities in many other southern cities – that sympathized with the plight of southern blacks.

The Durrs knew Parks personally as they had hired her on a regular basis as a seamstress to alter their daughter's dresses. They accompanied Nixon to the police station, where Nixon signed the bail bond for Parks's release. Enthusiastic about using the incident as a legal test case, Nixon told Parks, 'With your permission we can break down segregation on the bus[es].'

Women's Political Council: Women's civil rights group in Montgomery, Alabama, headed by teacher Jo Ann Robinson, which played an important role in organizing the Montgomery bus boycott.

Fred Gray meanwhile contacted Jo Ann Robinson, president of the **Women's Political Council (WPC)**, about the Parks incident. The WPC was made up of a small number of black women educators, all of whom were affiliated with Montgomery's black Alabama State College. In its relatively short life the WPC had established itself as one of the most active political groups in the city. Robinson had spearheaded previously unsuccessful attempts to petition the city to alter segregation practices on buses after previous incidents [Doc. 6, p. 138]. Gray and Robinson had held 'many discussions . . . with reference to what should be done in the event another incident occurred'.

Robinson contacted Nixon, and both agreed that the Parks case offered the possibility of mobilizing the black community in a united protest at her treatment. They agreed that a mass meeting should be organized to engage the support of the black community, and that a one-day bus boycott should be organized for the following Monday. Nixon took the job of making the necessary arrangements for the mass meeting and Robinson, along with other members of the WPC, made leaflets reading 'Don't ride the bus to work, to town, or any place Monday December 5' and began to distribute them in the black community.

Parks's refusal to surrender her seat was not the first time a black person in Montgomery had challenged treatment by whites on a city bus. Ten years earlier Geneva Jordan had been arrested for 'talking back' to a white driver. Since then, Viola White, Katie Wingfield, and two children visiting from the state of New Jersey, had all been arrested for sitting in the section of the bus reserved for whites. In 1952, a city policeman shot dead a black man who argued with a bus driver over the correct fare. The following year, Epsie

Worthy was fined after a fracas with a bus driver in another fare dispute. In 1955, in the months leading up to Parks's arrest, both Claudette Colvin and Mary Louise Smith had been arrested for refusing to move to the back of the bus.

Neither was it the first time that a southern black community had organized a bus boycott to protest against segregation. In 1953, Rev. Theodore J. Jemison had done the same thing in **Baton Rouge**, Louisiana. Utilizing taxis and then a car pool as alternative transportation systems for black passengers, the boycott lasted for ten days until whites finally acquiesced in black demands to modify segregation practices.

Baton Rouge Bus Boycott: A 1953 bus boycott in Louisiana that preceded the more famous 1955–1956 Montgomery bus boycott.

But the Rosa Parks case was different for a number of reasons. Parks was a well-respected community figure and a seasoned activist. Montgomery's black community, which at around 42,750 people represented over a third of the city's total population, and accounted for over 70 per cent of bus passengers, was large enough to make an impact with a bus boycott. At the same time, the black community was relatively small and compact enough to coordinate such a protest effectively. Montgomery also possessed more than its fair share of able black leaders and existing black organizations that were ready and able to mobilize the black population.

The 1954 *Brown* decision swung the legal initiative over desegregation towards the black community and added further leverage to its demands. Just as importantly, the way in which the city's white power structure handled the bus boycott did much to contribute to its success. Making a series of tactical blunders, Montgomery's white leaders escalated rather than dissipated the boycott at critical points in its development.

King only became involved in the developing protest movement in Montgomery when E. D. Nixon telephoned him to ask if Dexter could be used as the venue for a mass meeting to discuss Rosa Parks's arrest and to make plans for a bus boycott. At first, King hesitated. He did not want to get too deeply involved in what was bound to be a controversial protest. King's good friend and fellow city pastor Rev. Ralph D. Abernathy called to urge his help. King agreed to hold the meeting at Dexter on the evening of 2 December 1955, whilst insisting he could not take a significant leadership role. At the meeting, it was agreed that a boycott should begin the following Monday.

The first signs on Monday morning were encouraging. King watched nearly empty buses pass by his window, counting only eight black passengers over the course of an hour. The same day, it took an all-white jury just five minutes to find Rosa Parks guilty as charged. Several hundred blacks turned up at the courthouse that morning, providing an unprecedented and highly visible degree of community support for Parks's action.

Later that afternoon, black leaders met to discuss what to do next. Three demands were put forward. Firstly, the implementation of modified segregated seating arrangements on buses. There was no demand for total bus desegregation, which blacks knew the city would reject outright. Secondly, that white bus drivers should treat black passengers with courtesy. Thirdly, that blacks should be allowed to apply for the job of bus driver.

Montgomery Improvement Association: A coalition of organizations that joined together to run the 1955–1956 Montgomery bus boycott.

The meeting then agreed to form a **'Montgomery Improvement Association' (MIA)** to take charge of the bus boycott. But there remained the delicate question of who should lead it. None of the established leaders in the community wanted their rivals to dominate the organization. Finally, King was put forward as a compromise candidate. As a relative newcomer to, and a junior member of, the black community, he appeared to be no threat to any of the existing community leaders.

There were other reasons behind the choice of King for president. The fact that he was a minister was crucial. Since the church congregation funded his job, King was able to head the MIA with more impunity than someone like Jo Ann Robinson, who, as a black teacher, was reliant on white state funding for her salary. For blacks in public employment, antagonizing whites almost automatically meant being fired. A minister was also a good choice of leader because he had access to a church, one of the few places where the black community could hold mass meetings to rally support for the boycott. Moreover, a minister's link to a black congregation placed him at the head of an important information network within the black community. As head of the church, a minister could help to sway his members to support the boycott and lend sanction and authority to it.

King fulfilled these and two other important criteria. Firstly, he was one of the few ministers actually willing to accept the role. Many black ministers initially preferred to stay out of the controversy because they were doubtful of its potential success and because they did not want to become a target for white anger. Secondly, King's congregation contained many influential members of Montgomery's black middle class. Their inclusion would unite the black community and, on a purely practical level, provide the boycott with a supply of automobiles for alternative transportation. 'I'm not sure I'm the best person for this position,' King told the meeting, 'but if no one else is going to serve, I'd be glad to try.'

Little more than twenty minutes later, King delivered his first speech as MIA president at Holt Street Baptist Church. Firstly, King asserted the right to protest against the treatment of blacks on city buses, citing the US Supreme Court, the US Constitution, and 'God Almighty' as supporters of their cause. Secondly, King told the audience that they should stick together, that they should not be afraid, and that at all times they must keep 'God in the forefront. Let us be Christian in all our actions.' Love and justice, not hatred of whites, should be their guiding principle, King insisted.

Finally, King framed the bus boycott in epic terms, telling the audience that 'when the history books are written in the future, somebody will have to say "There lived a race of people, a black people . . . who had the moral courage to stand up for their rights. And thereby they injected a new meaning into the veins and history of civilization."' The crowd of 1,000 people inside and 4,000 gathered outside roared their approval of continuing with the boycott.

Montgomery's white authorities were taken aback by the show of support for the bus boycott and the decision to continue the protest. Montgomery mayor William A. Gayle unsuccessfully met with MIA and bus company representatives in an effort to broker a compromise. The total inflexibility of the bus company took the MIA by surprise, but it also strengthened its members' resolve to press home their demands. So too did other efforts to intimidate the black community. White newspaper the *Montgomery Advertiser* noted an obscure section of state law that forbade boycotts. Montgomery police commissioner Clyde C. Sellers pointed to a city ordinance that required all taxicabs to charge a minimum fare, which would strip the boycott of its alternative transportation arrangements for the city's black population. The MIA organized a car pool instead.

At the beginning of 1956, the situation polarized further. The MIA began to discuss the possibility of filing a court suit to seek the complete desegregation of city buses. At the same time the city announced a new 'get tough' policy. City police began to disperse blacks when they gathered at car pool meeting points and to harass black car pool drivers with tickets for minor offences. On Thursday 26 January, city policemen arrested King for travelling at 30 miles per hour in a 25 miles per hour speed zone. Hauled off to jail, King was fingerprinted and locked up in a squalid communal cell.

Although King spent only a short time in jail before being released, the arrest shook him. The episode brought home the full weight of the task that he had taken on in agreeing to become MIA president and the implications of that decision for himself and his family. The longer the bus boycott continued, the more likely it was that King would become the focus for white hostility. 'Almost every day', King recalled, 'someone warned me that he had overheard white men making plans to get rid of me.'

When he arrived home from jail, King received another of the anonymous threatening telephone calls from whites that he and other MIA members had been subjected to since the boycott began. 'Nigger, we are tired of you and your mess now,' said the caller. 'And if you are not out of town in three days, we're going to blow your brains out and blow up your house.'

Later that night, unable to sleep, King sat in his kitchen over a cup of coffee and pondered his future. He wondered if he could find a discreet way to back out of his leadership role without appearing to be a coward. At his lowest ebb since the boycott began, and racked with doubt, King prayed for guidance: 'I am here taking a stand for what I believe is right. But now I am afraid. The people are looking to me for leadership, and if I stand before them without strength and courage, they too will falter. I am at the end of my powers. I have nothing left. I've come to the point where I can't face it alone.'

In prayer, King heard an inner voice telling him not to give up. 'Stand up for righteousness,' the voice said. 'Stand up for truth; and God will be at your side forever.' King always believed that the episode constituted a personal religious revelation and calling which he had never truly experienced before. So strong was its impact that it immediately assuaged his doubts and fears and left him more determined than ever to continue on as MIA president.

Just a few nights later segregationists carried out their threat and bombed King's home with his wife Coretta and their two-month-old daughter Yolanda inside. King rushed home from Dexter where he was preaching. Several hundred black onlookers as well as the city police were at his home. To King's relief, no one had been injured by the blast, but the front room windows were shattered and there was a sizeable hole blown in the concrete porch outside.

The day after the bombing, MIA attorney Fred Gray filed suit against the city in federal court under the title of **Browder v. Gayle**. The suit demanded an end to the harassment of car pool drivers and challenged the constitutional basis of segregation on Montgomery buses. With all prospect of a negotiated settlement having vanished, the MIA leadership decided that only the courts could now settle the issue.

Browder v. Gayle (1956): US District Court case that led to the desegregation of buses in Montgomery.

The decision to launch a new lawsuit, independent of Rosa Parks's case, which was already on appeal in the courts, sprang from a desire to untangle the specifics of the Parks case from the general principle of challenging segregation. Therefore, it was not Parks's name, but those of other volunteer plaintiffs that were attached to the case.

The city authorities responded to the MIA lawsuit with mass indictments of MIA members for breaking the state's anti-boycott laws. On 20 March 1956, in agreement with the prosecuting and defence attorneys, King was the first member of the MIA to be tried under the state's anti-boycott law. As expected, three days later King was found guilty. He was fined $500 and ordered to pay $500 court costs. MIA attorneys announced that they would appeal against the decision. With the appeal process expected to take the best part of a year, the trials of the other 88 MIA members were held in abeyance until the higher courts reviewed King's case.

On 11 May 1956, a special three-judge federal court panel in Montgomery heard the MIA's case. On 5 June, the court ruled against segregation on city buses. The city announced that it would appeal the case to the US Supreme Court. Finally, on 17 December, the US Supreme Court rejected the city's appeal. On 20 December, the order to desegregate buses was served on city officials. The next morning, at 5.45 a.m., King was one of the first people to ride an integrated bus.

Initial peaceful compliance quickly turned into a violent backlash. In the early morning of 23 December, someone fired a shotgun blast through King's front door. On 28 December, white snipers firing at a city bus wounded black passenger Rosa Jordan who was eight months pregnant. On 10 January 1957, four black churches were bombed in a coordinated attack. Only a vigilant night watchman prevented the bombing of King's church. On 27 January, a bomb destroyed the home of black hospital worker Allen Robertson, who lived just a few hundred yards from King's parsonage. A second disarmed bomb was found at the parsonage. Though arrests were made no convictions were ever secured.

City buses, nevertheless, remained desegregated. Crucially, the boycott had demonstrated the ability of a united black community to defy segregation peacefully and to thereby overcome it. In doing so, blacks found a new self-confidence and new self-respect in the face of white efforts to intimidate them.

When 40 Ku Klux Klan cars drove through black Montgomery on the night of the decision to desegregate city buses, the Klansmen expected the usual black response of silence, fear and retreat. Instead, King reported, 'the Negroes behaved as though they were watching a circus parade. Concealing the effort it took them, they walked about as usual; some simply watched from their steps; a few waved at the passing cars. After a few blocks, the Klan, nonplussed, turned off into a sidestreet and disappeared into the night.'

A black janitor in Montgomery told a white northern reporter, 'We got our heads up now, and we won't ever bow down again – no, sir – except before God!' Moreover, the bus boycott had a regional, even national resonance among blacks. As James Forman, later executive secretary of SNCC wrote, the 'Montgomery bus boycott had a very significant effect on the consciousness of black people throughout the United States'. Many others who joined later demonstrations were, like Forman, affected and inspired by the boycott.

Yet despite the stirred emotions it gave rise to, the bus boycott's practical impact on the civil rights struggle remained unclear. Did the boycott represent a unique, one-off development in a particular locality? Could the Montgomery model of protest be successfully repeated elsewhere? What of Martin Luther King, Jr.? Was he just a talented local leader or could he build upon his newfound national standing to establish himself as a regional, even national black leader? During the years after the Montgomery bus boycott, King and other civil rights activists sought to address and answer these questions.

Further reading

Accounts by participants in the boycott, alongside King's *Stride Toward Freedom*, include Rosa Parks, with Jim Haskins, *Rosa Parks: My Story* (1992); Jo Ann Robinson, with David Garrow, *The Montgomery Bus Boycott and the Women Who Started It* (1989); and Fred D. Gray, *Bus Ride to Justice: Changing the System by the System: The Life and Works of Fred D. Gray, Preacher, Attorney, Politician, Lawyer for Rosa Parks* (1999). A useful collection of primary documents on the boycott is Stewart Burns, ed., *Daybreak of Freedom: The Montgomery Bus Boycott* (1997). The larger story of southern transportation desegregation is told in Catherine Barnes, *Journey From Jim Crow: The Desegregation of Southern Transit* (1983).

4

The Southern Christian Leadership Conference (SCLC), 1957–1960

In the years immediately following the Montgomery bus boycott, King's youth (he was still only 26 when the Montgomery bus boycott ended) and inexperience was telling. He was intimidated by his newfound responsibilities, confessing to one family friend, J. Pious Barbour, that he was 'worried to death. A man who hits the peak at twenty-seven has a tough job ahead. People will be expecting me to pull rabbits out of the hat for the rest of my life.'

Nevertheless, appearances with established black leaders, black celebrities, and white politicians, only confirmed King's status as an emerging symbol of a developing new black movement in the United States. In May 1957, King spoke at a 'Prayer Pilgrimage for Freedom' at the Lincoln Memorial in Washington DC, sharing the platform with A. Philip Randolph and NAACP executive secretary Roy Wilkins.

King's speech, 'Give Us the Ballot', emphasized the importance of black voting rights over non-violent direct action [**Doc. 7, p. 139**]. Like many other black leaders, King believed that 'If the Negro achieved the ballot throughout the South, many of the problems which we faced would be solved.' But the fact that King had little new to say did not deter black *Amsterdam News* reporter James Hicks writing that King was now 'the number one leader of sixteen million Negroes in the United States'.

In October 1958 and again in April 1959, Randolph invited King to speak at a 'Youth March for Integrated Schools' in the nation's capital. In June 1957, King and Ralph Abernathy met privately with Vice President Richard M. Nixon. A year later, President Dwight D. Eisenhower agreed to meet with King and a delegation of other black leaders at the White House.

Two trips abroad confirmed that King was not just a national, but also an international, symbol of black America. On 5 March 1957, King and his wife, Coretta, along with other black leaders from the United States, attended the independence ceremonies marking the transfer of power from the British colony of the Gold Coast to the Republic of Ghana.

The trip, King's first outside of the United States, provided a global context within which to locate the unfolding struggle back home. 'I thought it [Ghanaian independence] would have worldwide implications and repercussions,' King later reflected, 'not only for Asia and Africa, but also for America . . . I thought Ghana would become a symbol of hope for hundreds and thousands of oppressed peoples all over the world as they struggled for freedom.' In the midst of their travels, the Kings' second child, Martin Luther King III, was born on 23 October 1957.

In February and March 1959, King, Coretta and Lawrence D. Reddick, a history professor at Alabama State College and a friend of the Kings, visited India at the invitation of the Gandhi National Memorial Fund. In India, King met with many of Gandhi's compatriots, including Prime Minister Jawaharlal Nehru. India's attempts to overcome the centuries of injustice inflicted by the caste system provided King with another instructive parallel for attempts by blacks in the United States to overcome second-class citizenship there. King noted that 'India appeared to be integrating its untouchables faster than the United States was integrating the Negro community. . . . I left India more convinced than ever before that nonviolent resistance was the most potent weapon available to oppressed people in their struggle for freedom.'

King's prominence brought its own problems. With the bus boycott over, both old and new rivalries began to surface in Montgomery's black community. King had initially been chosen to head the MIA in part because he was not perceived as posing a threat to existing black leaders, and because he was not involved in their squabbles. Subsequent events meant that King's star rose higher than other black leaders in the city. Media accounts placed him at the centre of the boycott. Even though King's own account of the Montgomery bus boycott, published as *Stride Toward Freedom: The Montgomery Story* in 1958, was at pains to acknowledge the efforts of other, many still felt that the young preacher was unjustly emphasizing his role in events while diminishing theirs.

MIA members became disgruntled. E. D. Nixon left to pursue his own voter registration campaign and asked Rosa Parks, who felt excluded from the MIA, to join him. There were tensions between lawyer Fred Gray and others MIA members. Rev. Uriah J. Fields, the MIA's recording secretary, resigned to form the Restoration and Amelioration Association as a rival to the MIA.

With all the in-fighting, the MIA failed to make progress in addressing the needs of the black community. Its first post-boycott project of forming a credit union for Montgomery blacks met with little success. When the MIA launched a lawsuit to desegregate city parks it did manage to win a favourable court ruling. However, the city responded by closing all of the public parks for blacks and whites alike. This hurt blacks more, since many well-to-do whites had access to private park facilities.

Plans to launch a legal challenge to continuing segregation in Montgomery's public schools brought the threat from incoming Alabama governor John Patterson to close all of the city's public schools rather than to desegregate them. As with the parks, this would disadvantage the black population more, since whites would have better access to private schools. Moreover, there were worries among the city's black teachers that the closure of black public schools would lead to job losses. In light of this, the MIA put its plans to challenge school desegregation on hold.

King's difficulties in dealing with local black leaders were echoed at the national level. In particular, he found himself in conflict with NAACP leader Roy Wilkins. Wilkins was wary of King, who appeared far better at reaching out to and communicating with the black masses than he did. Moreover, King and Wilkins placed a different emphasis on the future of the black struggle for civil rights. Although both agreed that litigation and legislation would form an important basis for gaining equal rights, Wilkins did not accept that the use of non-violent direct action had any significant role to play.

King's experience with the Montgomery bus boycott convinced him that non-violent direct action, working alongside litigation and legislation, would be necessary in the fight against segregation. Wilkins feared that King and the SCLC were trying to usurp not only the NAACP's influence over the future direction of the movement but also, with far-reaching consequences for the very existence of the NAACP, its membership and donations. King was at pains to placate Wilkins and the NAACP and tried to convince them that the SCLC would work alongside and not in competition with them. Such assurances, however, did little to assuage Wilkins's ongoing doubts.

King's arrest in September 1958 demonstrated that although he could mix with national and international dignitaries, back in his home state and in much of the South the white population considered him public enemy number one. King was back in Montgomery to attend the trial of Edward Davis, who had attacked Ralph Abernathy in his church office after accusing him of having an affair with his wife. When King and Coretta tried to enter the courtroom, the police refused to admit them. King told them he was waiting to see his lawyer, Fred Gray, who was there to assist Abernathy. When King peered into the courtroom to try to attract Gray's attention a nearby police sergeant took offence, telling him 'Boy, you done done it now.'

King was placed under arrest for loitering. The next morning, he was summarily tried and convicted and handed a $14 fine or a 14-day prison sentence. For the first time, drawing upon his growing understanding of non-violent methods of protest, King refused to pay the fine and accepted imprisonment to draw attention to the injustice of his arrest.

King's arrest and his decision to go to jail temporarily rekindled the community spirit of the bus boycott in Montgomery. Abernathy marched the crowd waiting outside the courtroom to King's church and made plans to hold a vigil outside the jail. However, in a wholly unexpected development, King was refused entry into prison. Alert to the fact that King's incarceration could potentially reunite the black community, police commissioner Clyde Sellers paid King's $14 fine himself. The irony of this event was made light of at a mass meeting afterwards, but it contained an ominous warning that law enforcement officers were learning quickly about how to counter non-violent protest tactics.

Another warning about the perils of prominence came the following month when a black woman, Izola Ware Curry, stabbed King in the chest with a Japanese letter opener as he signed copies of his book *Stride Toward Freedom* in New York City. Curry casually came up to King and asked 'Are you Martin Luther King?' King replied 'Yes.' Curry then plunged the letter opener into his chest. The blade lodged perilously close to his heart and required delicate surgery to remove. Even a slight movement between the store and the hospital might have killed him. 'If you had sneezed,' King's doctor later told him, 'your aorta would have been punctured and you would have drowned in your own blood.'

Curry's incoherence at the trial led to her diagnosis as a paranoid schizophrenic and she was admitted indefinitely to a state hospital for the criminally insane. King's period of recovery after the stabbing offered some respite from a relentless schedule. Between marches, meetings, speaking engagements and overseas visits, King spent long periods away from home.

Surviving a life-threatening injury only convinced King of his call to leadership. 'I was intensely impatient to get back to continue the work we all knew had to be done regardless of the cost,' he reported. 'I did not have the slightest intention of turning back.' Family commitments and his duties as a pastor increasingly came second to his new responsibilities as a leader in the civil rights struggle.

Despite his expenditure of time and energy, King failed to maintain the momentum of the bus boycott in Montgomery and to expand black activism across the South and the nation. Progress on civil rights still lagged. Although President Eisenhower sent federal troops to enforce the integration of Central High School in Little Rock, Arkansas, in September 1957, such federal intervention proved the exception rather than the rule. School desegregation met with widespread resistance in the South and made painfully slow progress, or none at all.

Civil Rights Act of 1957: First civil rights act since Reconstruction, which established the Department of Justice Civil Rights Division.

The **Civil Rights Act** passed by the US Congress in September 1957 was a move in the right direction – it had been 82 years since the last one – but it ultimately provided only token legislation. Opposition from southern congressmen such as South Carolina senator Strom Thurmond, who held the senate floor by **filibustering** for over 24 hours to stall action on the bill, meant that many of its original provisions, such as empowering the **Justice Department** to sue for the enforcement of school desegregation, were struck down. White resistance looked like it might put a stop to the embryonic black protest movement before it had even had a chance to get off the ground.

King sought to strengthen the movement and to give it greater coherence by helping to form a new civil rights organization. He was assisted by three key people in this task: Bayard Rustin, Ella Baker and Stanley Levison.

Rustin, from Pennsylvania, had a long and varied career as a social and political activist. He had belonged to the Young Communist League and the US Socialist Party; he assisted A. Philip Randolph organize the March on Washington Movement in 1941; he had helped James Farmer in setting up CORE in 1942; and he had participated in CORE's 1947 '**Journey of Reconciliation**'. Rustin had also played a short but influential advisory role to King during the Montgomery bus boycott by tutoring King in non-violence. However, revelations about Rustin's background in radical politics and his homosexuality forced him to leave sooner than expected.

Baker, from North Carolina, worked with the New Deal agency the Works Progress Administration in the 1930s before joining the national office of the NAACP as national field secretary. She later became the NAACP's director of branches. In the course of her work, Baker met with many black activists across the South, as well as US Communist Party members and other left-wing activists.

One of Baker's contacts was Stanley Levison, a white Jewish New Yorker who was a trained lawyer and who had previously been involved with groups such as the **American Jewish Congress** and the NAACP. It was through the NAACP that Levison met Baker. Like Baker and Rustin, and many other social and political activists of the time, Levison moved in left-wing circles and was a former communist sympathizer.

Rustin, Baker and Levison urged King to think about how to expand the Montgomery example of black activism. They persuaded him that any new civil rights organization formed to do this should be completely independent of other organizational ties and have distinct goals and a new vision of its own.

On 10 and 11 January 1957, King convened a meeting in Atlanta to discuss the matter. The 60 or so respondents who attended that meeting agreed, based upon working papers provided by Rustin and Baker, to establish a temporary 'Southern Leadership Conference on Transportation and Nonviolent Integration'. At a further meeting organized by Rustin in New Orleans on 14 February, it was agreed to establish a permanent organization. Finally, in August, at its first annual convention, the group changed its name to the

Filibustering: Talking at length to hold the floor of an assembly to prevent a vote from taking place.

Justice Department: The US Department of Justice is the federal executive department that enforces the law and administers justice.

Journey of Reconciliation: Testing of desegregated interstate buses initiated by FOR in 1947.

American Jewish Congress: Lobby group for Jewish interests, based in the United States.

Southern Christian Leadership Conference (SCLC) with the conference theme providing the motto of the organization: 'To Redeem the Soul of America'.

SCLC had a number of distinctive hallmarks. Firstly, it was largely composed of and led by southern blacks. This meant that it had a strong indigenous base in the South. This, in turn, addressed Rustin's concern that the new organization should be different from existing civil rights organizations in distancing itself more from white, middle-class, northern intellectuals and liberals. An organization led by and for southern blacks, and especially led by black ministers (although Rustin had opposed the addition of 'Christian' to SCLC's title, fearing that it could alienate non-religious members) increased the likelihood of black support for the organization.

Secondly, the involvement of Rustin, Baker and Levison helped to bring on board the support of A. Philip Randolph, which they considered essential. As one of black America's most respected leaders, Randolph lent credibility and respectability to the SCLC and provided an important source of political and financial support from the labour movement. Moreover, as a known staunch anti-communist, Randolph's support signalled to others that the SCLC was a mainstream organization free from subversive or radical intent, an important criterion in the context of Cold War America.

Thirdly, the way that the SCLC was structured was also significant, especially in its self-conscious differentiation from the NAACP. Each affiliate group paid a $25 subscription that entitled it to a certificate of affiliation, the right to send five delegates to the SCLC annual convention, and to seek advice and assistance from SCLC staff members. Importantly, unlike the NAACP, the SCLC did not solicit individual memberships. Indeed, the way that the SCLC was set up allowed its members to remain in the NAACP – many SCLC members were NAACP local and state presidents – and sought to placate the older civil rights organization by demonstrating that both organizations could work side-by-side in the South.

The SCLC had a governing board of 33 people. All board members were black, two-thirds of them were preachers (with a preponderance of Baptists), all were from the urban South, and most were relatively well-off members of the black upper middle class. There was just one female member on the board.

The main thrust of the SCLC's direction and focus came from black southern preachers and especially from King, who was elected SCLC president, and remained in that position for the rest of his life. From the outset, King was absolutely synonymous with the SCLC, which in effect became his own personal vehicle for civil rights leadership. Board members mostly rubber-stamped all of King's nominees, suggestions, statements and actions.

Once launched, the SCLC was painfully slow in moving into action. It took almost all of 1957 to establish its structure and organizational procedures. The SCLC's first campaign was an attempt to expand the Montgomery bus boycott model of protest to other cities. For a variety of reasons this failed. In New Orleans, Atlanta and Mobile, white city authorities complied with court-ordered desegregation to forestall the development of a mass movement. In Miami, blacks represented too small a proportion of the population to make a bus boycott effective. In Birmingham, 'police intimidation, poor planning, black disunity, and the problem of devising alternative transportation' were all obstacles.

Only in two places did a sustained bus boycott emerge. In Tallahassee the boycott failed to achieve a clear victory. In Rock Hill, South Carolina, a six-month boycott put the bus company out of business completely. These disparate developments appeared to indicate that the success of the Montgomery bus boycott was a unique, one-off occurrence.

Faced with this setback, the SCLC shifted its focus to what it thought would be the more promising endeavour of voter registration. Such a campaign coincided with the civil rights bill being debated by Congress in 1957 that included a proposal to tackle voting discrimination. The SCLC believed there would be less white opposition to voter registration than to desegregation, since it did not raise the sensitive issue of racial mixing. A voter registration drive also offered a way to unite SCLC affiliates in a coordinated regional programme.

In July 1957, Rustin and Levison drew up a plan for an SCLC voter registration campaign. This included raising $200,000 to set up a central office in Atlanta with an executive director and a staff of field workers. The team of workers would then help to set up voter registration committees that would hold voting clinics to encourage blacks to register to vote and collect evidence of black disenfranchisement. Ella Baker launched the '**Crusade for Citizenship**' on 12 February 1958 from SCLC's Atlanta headquarters. In May, Rev. John L. Tilley from Baltimore joined her as the SCLC's first executive director.

Crusade for Citizenship: Early and largely unsuccessful SCLC voter registration campaign launched in 1958.

The SCLC's second campaign, however, proved little more successful than the first. The planned extensive network of voter registration committees failed to materialize, as did the overly ambitious funding target. In April 1959, King fired SCLC executive director Tilley, citing the lack of a 'dynamic program commensurate with the amount of money' spent. Baker was given the job of acting executive director.

The SCLC's Atlanta headquarters remained essentially a one-woman operation, with Baker left to coordinate the Crusade for Citizenship, to make field trips, to prepare SCLC's newsletter, to arrange conventions and board meetings, to make reports to King and the SCLC's administrative committee, and to compile complaints about voting discrimination. Finally, exasperated at being left to do all of the work and at the continuing lack of a strategy and direction within the organization, in October 1959 Baker challenged King and the board of directors to re-examine the way that the SCLC operated.

The review produced a number of important changes. The SCLC stream-lined its operations, reduced the number of board meetings and conventions, appointed a smaller subcommittee to assist Baker, and planned greater diversity of aims and goals in its future activities. King also addressed the growing concern that he personally was not devoting enough attention to the development of the SCLC by resigning his post at Dexter and moving to Atlanta to share the pastorate of Ebenezer Baptist Church with his father. This freed King from the obligation to preach every Sunday, it put him in the same city as the SCLC's headquarters, and it placed him in the city that was a major transportation hub for the South, making it easier and quicker for him to reach appointments around the country.

On 31 January 1960, King said goodbye to the Dexter congregation, explaining that 'History has thrust something upon me from which I cannot turn away.' Just one day later, history thrust another direct challenge to King, as a new student sit-in movement stole the initiative and lurched the civil rights struggle into its next phase. King again found himself playing catch-up and responding to events set in motion by others.

Further reading

The best studies of the SCLC are Adam Fairclough, *To Redeem the Soul of America: The Southern Christian Leadership Conference and Martin Luther King, Jr.* (1987) and David J. Garrow, *Bearing the Cross: Martin Luther King, Jr. and the Southern Christian Leadership Conference* (1986). Of the SCLC's founders, there is no biography of Stanley Levison, but both Ella Baker and Bayard Rustin have dedicated studies. On Baker see Joanne Grant, *Ella Baker: Freedom Bound* (1998) and Barbara Ransby, *Ella Baker and the Black Freedom Movement: A Radical Democratic Vision* (2002). On Rustin see Jervis Anderson, *Bayard Rustin: Troubles I've Seen: A Biography* (1997); John D'Emillio, *Lost Prophet: The Life and Times of Bayard Rustin* (2003); and Daniel Levine, *Bayard Rustin and the Civil Rights Movement* (2000). For a collection of Rustin's writings see Bayard Rustin, Devon W. Carbado, and Donald Weise, eds., *Time on Two Crosses: The Collected Writings of Bayard Rustin* (2003). Useful autobiographies of two of King's closest SCLC confidants are Ralph David Abernathy, *And the Walls Came Tumbling Down* (1989) and Andrew Young, *An Easy Burden: The Civil Rights Movement and the Transformation of America* (1996).

Part 3

KING AND A DEVELOPING MOVEMENT, 1960–1963

5

Sit-ins and Freedom Rides, 1960–1961

Before King could make any impact on the SCLC's fortunes a new impetus for the civil rights movement came from elsewhere. The day after King delivered his farewell sermon in Montgomery, Ezell Blair, Jr., Franklin McCain, Joe McNeil and David Richmond, four black students at North Carolina Agricultural and Technical College in Greensboro, North Carolina, walked into a downtown Woolworths store. 'For about a week,' recalls Richmond, 'we four fellows sat around the A&T campus talking about the integration movement. And we decided to go down to Woolworths and see what would happen.'

The students bought a number of items in the store and then, keeping hold of their receipts, headed for the segregated lunch counter and ordered coffee. The waitress refused them service. They demanded to know why they could buy goods in other parts of the store, but not at the lunch counter, and refused to leave until they were given a satisfactory answer. The students stayed until the store closed. The next day, the four students returned with others from campus to resume the 'sit-in'.

Over the following days, more students joined them and began other sit-ins at other local stores. By the weekend, the stores had decided to close all of their lunch counters. The sit-ins forced the local white business community to address the question of whether segregation was worth the cost of racial unrest and the economic damage that it caused through loss of custom. Through sustaining pressure on them to act, the black students would eventually force white businessmen to relent and to desegregate downtown facilities.

Like the Montgomery bus boycott, the sit-ins were not without precedent. The tactic had been used decades before by labour unions. Between 1957 and 1960, at least 16 other cities had experienced similar demonstrations. However, what had been a fragmented, tentative, and experimental series of demonstrations in the late 1950s finally cohered in a region-wide movement in 1960.

In direct contrast to the Montgomery bus boycott, the 1960s sit-ins proved immediately exportable. The sit-ins expanded via an interrelated network of southern black colleges that could mobilize student-led action in other communities. Unlike bus boycotts, sit-ins did not require the mobilization of an entire community from the outset, and they were therefore much easier to organize and much simpler to instigate.

The week after the Greensboro sit-ins, other demonstrations occurred in different parts of North Carolina. They then spread to neighbouring states. Finally, they mushroomed across the South. From 1 February to 1 April, over 70 communities experienced sit-ins. By the end of 1960, over 70,000 students had participated in sit-ins or other forms of direct action, and there had been 3,600 arrests.

King first became involved with the sit-ins on 16 February when he addressed a meeting of students in Durham, North Carolina. The meeting was the idea of Rev. Doug Moore, a local black minister and SCLC board member. Moore, who had been involved in helping to organize earlier sit-in demonstrations in Durham, wanted students who had participated in sit-ins in North Carolina to establish formal and ongoing links between them. King encouraged the formation of such an organization in his address and passed on advice about how to conduct and how to develop the sit-ins.

As in the Montgomery bus boycott, King stressed the need for student protests to take place in a spirit of non-violence and to seek reconciliation with whites. He also encouraged students to supplement sit-ins with eco-

Jail not Bail: The tactic of remaining in jail rather than accepting bail as a form of protest.

nomic boycotts of stores and to pursue a '**Jail not Bail**' policy of choosing imprisonment over paying fines if convicted. At a later rally at White Rock Baptist Church, King assured black demonstrators that 'You have the full weight of the SCLC behind you in your struggle.'

It was SCLC's acting executive director Ella Baker who most enthusiastic-ally took on the task of supporting the sit-in movement. Baker wanted to extend Moore's idea of coordinating protests in North Carolina throughout the southern states. With $800 of SCLC money, Baker organized a conference at her alma mater, Shaw University, in Raleigh, North Carolina, on 15–17 April 1960. In the letter of invitation, the stated purpose of the conference was 'TO SHARE experience gained in recent protest demonstrations and TO HELP chart future goals for effective action' in order to build 'a more unified sense of direction for *training and action in Nonviolent Resistance*'.

From the outset, Baker was determined to safeguard the independence of the student movement from the influence of other organizations, particularly the SCLC. Already disillusioned with what she perceived to be King's falter-ing leadership, and on her way out of the SCLC, Baker wanted the students to form a new organization that would be more democratic and lean towards 'group-centered leadership' rather than the 'leader-centered group pattern of organization' that she felt hindered the SCLC with its 'prophetic leader [with] heavy feet of clay' [**Doc. 8, p. 139**].

A 'Temporary Student Nonviolent Coordinating Committee' was set up with Marion Barry, a Nashville, Tennessee student, elected chair. At further meetings held that year, students decided to drop the 'temporary' label and to make the Student Nonviolent Coordinating Committee (SNCC – pronounced 'snick') a permanent organization. SNCC remained closely bound to the SCLC. For the early part of its life, SNCC's headquarters was 'squeezed in one corner of the SCLC office' in Atlanta.

As the sit-in movement unfolded, King was involved in several uncomfortable brushes with the law. On 17 February 1960, two local deputy officers arrived at Ebenezer Baptist Church with warrants for King's arrest and for his extradition to Alabama. King faced two counts of perjury for allegedly falsely swearing to the accuracy of his 1956 and 1958 state tax returns. He went to Montgomery for arraignment and was released on $2,000 bond.

The arrest came as a complete shock. Alabama auditor Lloyd Hale had previously claimed that King's income was greater than King had reported. However, King thought the matter was resolved when he reluctantly agreed to pay $1,600 to dispel those accusations. The state of Alabama refused to let the matter rest, even though the case was the first time in the state's history that it had prosecuted anyone for perjury on a tax return. It was clearly a direct attempt to harass King and to besmirch his name.

King was particularly troubled by the allegations since they were directed at his personal integrity as a leader and insinuated that his main reason for involvement with the civil rights movement was for financial gain. In fact, quite the opposite was true. Throughout his career as a civil rights leader, King deliberately lived within modest means to avoid such allegations of corruption.

Nevertheless, the charges perturbed King and successfully diverted his energy and movement funds away from civil rights activities. In New York, Bayard Rustin and Stanley Levison set up a Committee to Defend Martin Luther King, chaired by A. Philip Randolph, and with Rustin as executive director. The committee began to raise money and to assemble a team of attorneys for King's defence.

When the trial began in Montgomery on 25 May 1960, the flimsy allegations of the state were quickly laid bare. On the witness stand, Lloyd Hale came close to admitting that the tax discrepancies highlighted by the state were easily explained, and that the outstanding sums were simply reimbursements to King for associated travel expenses. Various witnesses testified on matters ranging from King's good character to the intricacies of tax law.

To universal surprise, after hearing three days of testimony, an all-white southern jury rendered a fair verdict and took less than four hours to find King not guilty. Once again, Alabama's attempts to harass King backfired.

The allegations were proved false and the amount of money channelled into the Committee to Defend Martin Luther King demonstrated the extent of white liberal support for King and the civil rights movement in the North. The successful fund-raising exercise opened up new channels of financial support and provided a springboard to more effective money-raising efforts in the future.

Between his arrest and trial over alleged tax evasion, King was charged a second time over traffic violations. On the evening of 4 May, he and Coretta were driving their dinner guest, white writer Lillian Smith, back to her room at Emory University Hospital where she was receiving treatment. Police patrolmen, suspicious of the car's interracial occupancy, pulled King over. The officers discovered that King was driving a borrowed car with expired licence plates. Moreover, he had still not transferred his driving licence from Alabama to Georgia as state law required after 90 days' residence. After one of the police officers issued a citation, King was permitted to continue his journey.

On 23 September, King appeared before Judge J. Oscar Mitchell in DeKalb County. Mitchell dismissed the charge over expired licence plates but fined King $25 and imposed a twelve-month probation period for King's failure to obtain a valid Georgia driving licence. King paid the $25 immediately and put the seemingly innocuous incident out of mind.

The full ramifications of the traffic charge only became apparent later that October when King joined the sit-in movement in Atlanta. The sit-ins had reached Atlanta as early as March 1960, but conservative black leaders in the city, including King's father, Daddy King, urged caution and restraint. Without the wholehearted support of the adult black community the sit-in movement proceeded hesitantly and failed to achieve any breakthrough over the desegregation of downtown facilities.

By October, students were ready to take a more determined stand for desegregation. Three local student leaders, Lonnie King, Herschelle Sullivan and Julian Bond, asked King to join them on a sit-in. King was initially reluctant to comply with their request since he did not want to defy the influential Atlanta black elite and not least his own father. Yet, as the students pressed King hard, he realized that he had to 'practice what I preached' and agreed to join them.

The following morning, 19 October, King and 35 others were arrested at Rich's department store downtown for refusing to leave its segregated restaurant after being denied service. King and the others were taken to Fulton County Jail where they refused bail. The following days saw more demonstrations and further arrests, prompting the city's black and white leaders to enter into negotiations to end the protests. They reached an agreement to secure the release from jail of all the demonstrators. All, that is, except for King.

Judge Mitchell in DeKalb County wanted to assess King's case to determine whether his recent arrest violated the probation imposed after his earlier driving licence conviction. The following morning, King was taken from Fulton County Jail to appear before Mitchell. King's attorney, Donald L. Hollowell, had already filed an appeal against King's licence conviction and argued that his client could not be imprisoned until that hearing. Mitchell ignored Hollowell's argument, ignored King's plea that he did not realize that probationary terms were attached to the $25 fine, and ignored defence witnesses' pleas from Atlanta's black elite testifying to King's good character. Mitchell decided that King had broken the terms of his probation and handed him a four-month prison sentence.

Coretta and King's sister, Christine, both broke down in tears in the courtroom. Coretta was alarmed at the prospect of Martin going to jail while she was six months pregnant with their third child, Dexter Scott King. Only a phone call from Democratic presidential candidate John F. Kennedy to the local judge, in a speculative ploy to secure Kennedy black votes, brought about King's release from jail. Kennedy won a closely contested presidential election less than a month later.

In 1961, it was again developments outside of the control of King and the SCLC that stole the initiative in pushing forward the civil rights agenda. The Chicago-based civil rights organization CORE and its national director James Farmer initiated 'Freedom Rides' that year. In 1947, members of CORE had successfully travelled on an interracial 'Journey of Reconciliation' through a number of upper South states after the *Morgan* v. *Virginia* (1946) US Supreme Court ruling outlawed segregation on interstate bus routes. In *Boynton* v. *Virginia* (1960) the Supreme Court extended the *Morgan* ruling to include the desegregation of interstate bus terminal facilities.

Boynton v. **Virginia (1960):** US Supreme Court ruling that outlawed segregation in interstate bus terminals.

Farmer, in the wake of the sit-in movement and of increased civil rights activity across the South, proposed to renew the Freedom Rides to test facilities at bus terminals throughout the region. As with the sit-ins, creating a symbolic confrontation would, Farmer hoped, illustrate to the nation the ugly face of white southern bigotry that might even bring with it a federal response to the continued denial of civil rights. As Farmer put it 'Our philosophy was simple. We put on pressure and create a crisis so that they [federal government] react.'

On 4 May 1961, 13 Freedom Riders – three white women, three white men, and seven black men – divided into two groups and boarded Greyhound and Trailways buses in Washington DC. The first leg of their journey, through Virginia, North Carolina, South Carolina and Georgia, passed largely without incident. When they reached Atlanta, King and Wyatt Walker met with the riders, warning them that the next leg of their journey across Alabama would be the most difficult so far.

The two groups set off for Birmingham the next morning. At Anniston, Alabama, a white mob was waiting for the Greyhound bus armed with 'pistols, guns, blackjacks, clubs, chains, [and] knives'. The riders decided not to test facilities there but to move on. However, when they tried to leave, the mob slashed the bus's tyres. The bus limped out of Anniston before finally grinding to a halt on the outskirts of town with the mob still in pursuit. When someone threw a firebomb on board, the bus burst into flames and the riders had to evacuate.

One rider remembered 'yelling and screaming. They just about broke every window out of the bus . . . I really thought that that was going to be the end of me.' Initially, an undercover plain-clothes state investigator on board kept the white mob back with his revolver drawn, but as the riders poured out the mob began to attack them. Alabama state troopers belatedly arrived on the scene to escort the riders to Anniston Hospital.

An hour later, the Trailways bus pulled into Anniston, where three whites boarded, beat up several freedom riders, and physically forced the black riders into the back seats. They remained on board for the journey to Birmingham to make sure that the bus stayed segregated. Upon arrival in Birmingham, the Freedom Riders encountered an even more savage attack at the hands of members of the local Ku Klux Klan, who, in collusion with the local police force, were allowed a 15-minute beating of the riders before the law enforcement authorities intervened [**Doc. 9, p. 141**].

James Peck, a white freedom rider, recalled: 'This mob seized us and I was unconscious, I'd say, within a minute. I came to in an alleyway. Nobody was there. [Just] a big pool of blood.' Later, Birmingham's somewhat ironically titled public safety commissioner, who was in charge of the police department, Theophilus Eugene 'Bull' Connor, explained away the delayed arrival of his men by claiming that since it was Mother's Day there were fewer police on duty as he had allowed many of his officers the time off to spend with their families.

The riders on the Greyhound bus meanwhile found themselves still pursued by the white mob that lurked outside Anniston Hospital. Inside, the hospital authorities insisted that the Freedom Riders must leave, since the mob posed a threat to other patients. In Birmingham, SCLC contact Rev. Fred Shuttlesworth arranged a convoy to collect the Freedom Riders. Although Shuttlesworth insisted that those from his congregation who chose to participate in the errand of mercy should be non-violent, one noted that 'everyone of those cars had a shotgun in it'. The convoy made a successful recovery mission.

Despite all of the difficulties that they had encountered, the Freedom Riders were determined to continue their journey. However, bus drivers in Birmingham refused to transport them. The Freedom Riders therefore decided to abandon their overland journey and to proceed to New Orleans by plane. Even at the airport they were delayed by bomb threats. Only when US Attorney General Robert Kennedy sent John Seigenthaler, the only white southerner on his immediate staff, along to Birmingham to assist the Freedom Riders did they finally escape their ordeal.

Determined that the demonstration should not end in defeat, a group of students from Nashville, one of the leading sit-in movement centres, declared that they would continue the Freedom Ride. On 17 May, ten Nashville students arrived in Birmingham. When they tried to board a bus bound for Montgomery they were taken into 'protective custody' by local police. Held overnight and for much of the following day, eventually public safety commissioner Connor personally drove the students back to the state line, where he unceremoniously dumped them by the side of the road in the dead of night. The students were back in Birmingham by the following day. Yet white bus drivers again refused to carry them on the next leg of their journey to Montgomery.

Robert Kennedy finally intervened to break the impasse. He persuaded the bus company to take the students to Montgomery, telling local bus officials to contact 'Mr. Greyhound' to get them out of there if they had to. Robert Kennedy also secured a grudging assurance from Alabama governor John Patterson that the riders would be afforded state protection.

On 20 May, a Greyhound bus left Birmingham for Montgomery carrying the SNCC Freedom Riders with an escort of 16 Alabama highway patrol cars. When the buses approached Montgomery, the police escort disappeared. Downtown, a similar scene to the one previously played out in Birmingham occurred. John Doar, an assistant attorney general, witnessed events from a nearby payphone and relayed them direct to Robert Kennedy: 'The passengers are getting off . . . There are no cops. It's terrible . . . People are yelling "Get 'em, get 'em." It's awful.' Right at the centre of events, Nashville student John Lewis remembered: 'People came out of nowhere – men, women, children, with baseball bats, clubs, chains – and there was no police official around. They just started beating people' [**Doc. 9, p. 141**].

Local whites, as in Birmingham, were given 15 minutes to beat the Freedom Riders until the police arrived. Even John Seigenthaler, Robert Kennedy's administrative assistant, who was there simply as an observer, was beaten by the mob as he attempted to intervene. Infuriated that Governor Patterson had reneged on his promise to safeguard the riders, Robert Kennedy sent US federal marshals to Montgomery to protect them.

Ralph Abernathy arranged a meeting at his First Baptist Church the following evening to discuss events. King cancelled an engagement in Chicago to fly to Montgomery to attend. As the meeting began, a white mob gathered outside the church, trapping everyone inside. Federal marshals used tear gas in an attempt to disperse the mob. When the mob still refused to move, King made a personal call to Robert Kennedy.

Kennedy told King that the Alabama National Guard was on its way to provide the federal marshals with backup. Given Alabama's record of defending civil rights activists, the assurance did little to calm King. Even when the Alabama National Guard did arrive, the white mob still defiantly refused to leave. Not until 4.30 a.m. the following morning, after an all night siege, were the first of those inside the church escorted home.

The Nashville SNCC students still insisted that they would continue the Freedom Ride, even though King and James Farmer were reluctant to support them and the federal government openly opposed the plan. The students leaned heavily on King to accompany them on their journey, insisting that he had a moral responsibility to do so. To the great disappointment of the students, King refused, saying that his participation might violate his probation. King insisted that he would choose 'the where and when of [my] own **Golgotha**', a reference to the site of Christ's crucifixion.

On Wednesday, the first group of SNCC riders set off for Jackson, Mississippi, with a sizeable Alabama National Guard escort. A second bus set off later. Both made an uneventful journey to Jackson, where the students, as Robert Kennedy had arranged in advance with Mississippi governor James O. Eastland, were arrested when they attempted to use segregated facilities at the bus terminal. More civil rights activists from different parts of the country began to flood into Montgomery to take the ride to Jackson to join the Nashville students in jail. By the end of the summer, 328 Freedom Riders were in Mississippi jails.

CORE, along with the SCLC and SNCC, formed a **Freedom Rides Coordinating Committee (FRCC)** to orchestrate and to fund further Freedom Rides. President Kennedy warned King that 'This is not going to have the slightest effect on what the government is going to do.'

However, on 29 May, Robert Kennedy took up King's suggestion to petition the **Interstate Commerce Commission (ICC)**, an independent body that had direct responsibility for interstate travel facilities, to issue regulations to ban segregation. After holding hearings on the matter, the ICC issued a comprehensive ban on all forms of segregation in interstate transit and in interstate terminal facilities, effective from 1 November 1961. Although this took time to enforce, historian Catherine Barnes notes that 'By mid-1963, legacies of a **Jim Crow** transit structure lingered on, but . . . systematic discrimination in interstate transport had ended.'

In the wake of the sit-ins and the Freedom Rides, Martin Luther King, Jr.'s credibility as a civil rights leader was again on the line. His refusal to join the Freedom Rides dismayed SNCC students. Soon, they would be calling him 'de Lawd', part teasing and part mocking King for what they perceived as his

Golgotha: According to the Bible, the place of Christ's crucifixion.

Freedom Rides Coordinating Committee: A coalition of national civil rights organizations formed to orchestrate, coordinate and fund Freedom Rides over the summer of 1961.

Interstate Commerce Commission: Federal body that regulates commerce and transportation between US states.

Jim Crow: Named after a vaudeville character, the colloquial term given to southern segregation laws.

pomposity at likening himself to Christ. As King and the SCLC floundered and failed in their search for new direction, SNCC's brand of insistent and pressing non-violent direct action was dominating the movement. King understood the need to regain the initiative if he was to fulfil his role as a civil rights leader. An invitation from the local movement to join demonstrations in Albany, Georgia, in 1961, held out the prospect of doing this. Instead, it led to yet another embarrassing defeat for King.

Further reading

The most thorough and comprehensive treatment of the Greensboro sit-ins is William H. Chafe, *Civilities and Civil Rights: Greensboro, North Carolina and the Black Struggle For Freedom* (1980). On the influential Nashville group of sit-in students see David Halberstam, *The Children* (1998). Three key studies of SNCC have updated the scholarship on that organization over the decades: Howard Zinn, *SNCC: The New Abolitionists* (1965); Clayborne Carson, *In Struggle: SNCC and the Black Awakening of the 1960s* (1981); and Wesley C. Hogan, *Many Minds, One Heart: SNCC's Dream of a New America* (2007).

On the 1947 Journey of Reconciliation see Derek Charles Catsam, *Freedom's Main Line: The Journey of Reconciliation and the Freedom Rides* (2009). The definitive work on the 1961 Freedom Rides is Raymond Arsenault, *Freedom Riders: 1961 and the Struggle for Racial Justice* (2006). For the federal response see David Niven, *The Politics of Injustice: The Kennedys, The Freedom Rides, and the Electoral Consequences of a Moral Compromise* (2003). The best organizational study of CORE remains August Meier and Elliott Rudwick, *CORE: A Study in the Civil Rights Movement, 1942–1968* (1973). Two useful participant accounts are: James Farmer, *Lay Bare the Heart: an Autobiography of the Civil Rights Movement* (1985) and James Forman, *The Making of Black Revolutionaries* (1985)..

6

The Albany Campaign, 1961–1962

Albany, Georgia, would prove an important testing ground for King and the SCLC's evolving non-violent direct action strategy. There, King was drawn into a developing local movement with little advance planning. Conflicts of interest and bickering between the SCLC, SNCC, the NAACP and local leaders subsequently undermined black unity. Albany's white City Commission remained unmoved by black demands for change and refused to negotiate. Albany chief of police Laurie Pritchett made mass arrests instead of meeting demonstrations with force as Bull Connor had with the Freedom Rides, thus denying the movement any dramatic confrontation to leverage federal action.

A divided black movement, a unified white community and a largely unconcerned federal government meant that King and the SCLC were forced to retreat from Albany twice without gaining any concessions. Nevertheless, the Albany Campaign proved an important learning experience. It taught King and the SCLC a number of valuable lessons about what did and, more to the point, what did not work in running a community-based civil rights campaign. The defeat in Albany was a steep learning curve that helped to forge future tactics and successes.

Civil rights organizing in Albany began in 1961 when SNCC field secretary Charles Sherrod and SNCC volunteer Cordell Reagon sought to establish a voter registration campaign in south-west Georgia. Albany, where 26,000 blacks represented around 40 per cent of the city's 56,000 population, was a safer and more inviting base than surrounding rural areas in which to begin. Sherrod and Reagon began by canvassing student support for direct action. They hoped that this in turn would engage the support of Albany's black adult population. In anticipation of the ICC order to desegregate inter-state bus terminal facilities on 1 November, Sherrod and Reagon encouraged students to test facilities in Albany on that date.

The planned demonstrations encountered low-key policing which insistently moved them on but did not employ the levels of violence that Freedom

Riders had encountered in Alabama. This was largely down to Albany chief of police Laurie Pritchett. Pritchett had followed the development of the civil rights movement with keen interest and had 'researched Dr. King [and] read about his early days in Montgomery, his methods there'.

Pritchett had also witnessed the handling of the Freedom Rides in Alabama the previous year. He had observed that much of the success of non-violent direct action was down to the hostile and often violent reaction of whites to demonstrations. This convinced Pritchett that it would be best to handle demonstrations in Albany differently. He prepared his officers for demonstrations in advance and told them that there would be 'no violence, no dogs, no show of force . . . We're going to out-nonviolent them.'

King later noted that 'Pritchett felt that by directing his police to be non-violent, he had discovered a new way to beat [non-violent] demonstrations'. By forgoing explicitly brutal policing, and by instead arresting demonstrators on charges that did not raise the issue of segregation, such as obstruction and public order offences, Pritchett effectively contained the movement by denying it any publicity. Anticipating the use of 'jail not bail' tactics, Pritchett made contingency plans to use jails in surrounding counties if Albany's jails became overcrowded. He bargained, correctly as it turned out, on the movement running out of demonstrators before he ran out of jails [**Doc. 10, p. 142**].

The ongoing efforts of Sherrod and Reagon in Albany soon brought them into conflict with older members of the black community. The local NAACP branch felt that SNCC was poaching its own NAACP Youth Council recruits. The friction between SNCC and the NAACP led to the intervention of Albany's Criterion Club, a community organization of black professionals and businessmen. Three younger members of the Criterion Club, osteopath Dr William G. Anderson, attorney Chevene B. King, and his brother, estate agent Slater King, discussed developments in community meetings. They concluded that it would be best to work with SNCC representatives so that at the very least they could exert some control over them.

To that end, on 17 November they formed the **Albany Movement**. Like the MIA in Montgomery, the Albany Movement joined together a number of local black groups and leaders for the purpose of coordinating community protest efforts. Ambitiously, it decided to tackle racial discrimination on a number of fronts simultaneously, including demands for fair employment, an end to police brutality, and the desegregation of bus and train terminals and other city facilities. Anderson was elected president, with Slater King and Albany postal worker Marion S. Page making up a three-man coordinating committee.

Albany Movement: A coalition of organizations that joined together to run the 1961–1962 Albany Campaign.

Local NAACP president, dentist E. D. Hamilton, refused to sign up to the Albany Movement. Plans were made for three NAACP Youth Council members to independently test bus terminal facilities on 22 November. The three were arrested, along with two students with close links to SNCC, Bertha Gober and Blanton Hall. The arrested NAACP Youth Council members were released on bail, but Gober and Hall chose to go to jail instead. The movement's first mass meeting took place at Mount Zion Baptist Church three days later. All five students arrested at the bus terminal were handed 15 days' probation and $100 fines.

More demonstrations and arrests followed. Over 250 black students marched on City Hall in support for those arrested. They too were arrested. Despite Pritchett's best efforts to avoid publicity, the movement in Albany began to make national headlines as the scene of the 'first large-scale Negro uprising since the Montgomery bus boycott'. The reaction of the Albany Movement was twofold. Firstly, it began to exert economic pressure on Albany's white business community by organizing a boycott of city stores and city buses. Secondly, it invited outside help from the SCLC and asked King to come to Albany.

SNCC workers were unhappy with the decision to enlist outside help and saw 'no necessity for King to come'. They believed that local protest efforts were working sufficiently well already and that the self-confidence of local blacks was beginning to build. They were afraid that inviting King might introduce a 'Messiah complex' into the movement and that 'people would feel that only a particular individual could save them and would not move on their own to fight racism and exploitation'.

However, Dr Anderson was adamant about the need for King's help. He noted that the local movement had already run out of cash to bail local students out of jail. According to Anderson, SNCC 'provided what was needed – a stimulus – but once the movement got going they did not have the resources to manage the massive movement'. King was none too keen on going to Albany and getting sidetracked from his primary goal of building the SCLC into a regional force, but he finally agreed to put in a token appearance.

Concerned at the escalation of the protests in Albany and urged on by President Kennedy's civil rights assistant Burke Marshall, city authorities attempted to put a stop to the demonstrations. On 15 December, Albany mayor Asa D. Kelley announced that he was 'ready to . . . discuss all problems with responsible Negro leaders'. That afternoon, an informal biracial negotiating committee of three blacks not belonging to the Albany Movement (the city's definition of 'responsible leaders') and three whites met to discuss developments. The committee members agreed that if the city's train and bus terminal facilities desegregated and an ongoing biracial negotiating committee was formed to discuss further desegregation in Albany, the demonstrations would be halted.

King arrived in Albany that same evening and immediately found himself more embroiled than he had bargained for, when Dr Anderson invited King to march with him in Albany the following day. King's arrival soon polarized opinion in Albany. Whites refused to make concessions while pressured by his presence in the city and the local black community was even more emboldened in its demands because of it.

On 16 December, King and Anderson led over 250 people in a march to City Hall. Pritchett and his men blocked their way. When the marchers refused to disperse, Pritchett arrested them for parading without a permit and for obstruction. Anderson, King and Ralph Abernathy were separated from the rest of the marchers as they were taken into custody. Abernathy subsequently made bail to rally outside support. King told reporters: 'If convicted I will refuse to pay the fine. I expect to spend Christmas in jail. I hope thousands will join me.' Privately, he told confidants in the SCLC 'that we could not stay there more than three months. But if the sentences were less than three months we would serve the time.'

When Anderson and King were taken for trial on 19 December their hearings were postponed while new negotiations continued. A deal was reached that in exchange for a cessation of demonstrations and the departure of King from Albany, the city's bus and train terminals would be desegregated, the city would establish an eight-member biracial committee, and all local citizens would be released from jail. Mayor Kelley and Chief Pritchett gave their word on the settlement but refused to sign up to anything on paper. Despite reservations about this, the Albany Movement agreed to the deal.

The Albany Movement subsequently claimed victory. But Kelley and Pritchett insisted that no formal agreement existed. Moreover, Kelley noted to the press that Attorney General Robert Kennedy had already called him to congratulate the city on its handling of the crisis. Almost universally to onlookers it appeared that King had been outmanoeuvred and outwitted by Kelley and Pritchett. The *New York Herald Tribune* described Albany as a 'devastating loss of face' and a 'stunning defeat' for King. 'Segregation 1, King 0' read other headlines. Many reports focused upon and congratulated Pritchett on his policing methods and his strategy of 'neutralizing' non-violence by making mass arrests instead of using force.

Despite the criticism, King was in fact relieved to have been extricated from events in Albany. Refusing to dwell on the negative press, he returned to what he viewed as his central task of strengthening the SCLC. King briefly returned to Albany for trial on 27 February 1962 and was convicted on charges of disorderly conduct and for parading without a permit. Judge A. N. Durden, Sr. delayed sentencing and did not recall King for over five months. In King's absence, as SNCC workers had feared, Albany Movement leaders struggled to keep the local movement going.

On 10 July, King and Abernathy returned to Albany and were sentenced to 45 days in jail or a $178 fine. In an attempt to revive protests and to pressure the City Commission back to the negotiating table, they chose jail. King's jailing appeared to have the intended reinvigorating effect on the Albany Movement. The following day, 32 people took part in a downtown march. Pritchett arrested them all. A new round of demonstrations looked set to ignite.

Yet on the morning of 12 July, King and Abernathy were freed after it was claimed that a person unknown had paid their bail. In fact, King's release from jail was instigated by the city to prevent a re-emergence of demonstrations. King had little choice but to walk free. 'I've been thrown out of lots of places in my day,' Abernathy told a mass meeting afterwards, 'but never before have I been thrown out of jail.'

King announced a mass march for Saturday 21 July. In response, the city obtained a temporary restraining order from federal district judge J. Robert Elliott that forbade King and other named members of the Albany Movement from marching. Movement attorneys tried but failed to secure a vacation of the order. King called off the march, arguing that he could not disobey a federal court order since it would be inconsistent with the movement's demand that whites should obey federal laws that required desegregation.

On Tuesday morning, 24 July, movement attorneys successfully managed to get Judge Elliott's temporary restraining order vacated. Movement leaders used the decision to try to re-open negotiations with the city before launching new demonstrations. Earlier that day a sheriff in Mitchell County had beaten the pregnant Marion King, wife of Albany Movement leader Slater King, while she was visiting an arrested friend in jail. This inflammatory news threatened to strain appeals for non-violence.

However, a white CORE member from New York led a group of 40 marchers downtown. Pritchett arrested them all. Almost 2,000 black onlookers followed the progress of the march, fully expecting a confrontation with the police. Angered by the arrests, the black onlookers began to throw rocks and bottles. The missiles struck a city police officer and a state trooper. Pritchett used the outbreak of violence to question the movement's use of marches and the wisdom of the courts in allowing them to take place. Pritchett asked reporters if they had seen 'them nonviolent rocks'.

On 27 July, King led a delegation including Abernathy, Anderson and Slater King, to City Hall to request face-to-face talks with the City Commission. When they refused to leave they were arrested. A second group of 15 people led by SNCC's Charles Jones and William Hansen headed to City Hall several hours later. They too were arrested. Despite these new arrests, there were few other volunteers willing to go to jail. As SNCC had feared, many local blacks were becoming disillusioned with what they perceived as King's caution over pursuing further demonstrations.

Between Pritchett's successful policing tactics, the steadfast refusal of the City Commission to negotiate, the waning support of the black community,

Plate 1 The Montgomery bus boycott, 1955. Rosa Parks is fingerprinted after her arrest on a Montgomery bus, 1 December 1955.

© Pictorial Press Ltd/Alamy

Plate 2 Prayer Pilgrimage for Freedom, 17 May 1957. BSCPU president A. Philip Randolph, NAACP executive secretary Roy Wilkins, and Martin Luther King, Jr. receive the key to the city of Washington DC from Robert E. McLaughlin, President of the District Board of Commissioners.

© Bettmann/CORBIS

Plate 3 The March on Washington for Jobs and Freedom, 1963. A massive, peaceful, interracial assembly in Washington DC gave the civil rights movement mainstream credibility and showed that violence only occurred at civil rights demonstrations in the South because of hostile white actions.

© Flip Schulke/CORBIS

Plate 4 The Selma Campaign, 1965. SNCC chair John Lewis (today a Georgia US Congressman) is beaten by state troopers at Edmund Pettus Bridge in Selma, Alabama, on 'Bloody Sunday.' He was hospitalized with a fractured skull later that day.

© Bettmann/CORBIS

Plate 5 Burning buildings in Detroit after riots, 1967. 'Burn, Baby, Burn' became the rioters slogan in the 'long hot summers' between 1965 and 1967. Detroit was one of the many places hit. Such scenes prompted the establishment of the National Advisory Commission on Civil Disorders by President Lyndon B. Johnson in 1967.

© Bettmann/CORBIS

Plate 6 The Poor People's Campaign, May–June 1968. The Mule Train from Memphis to Washington DC brought the problems of the rural poor to the heart of American government, as shown in this striking juxtaposition of US Congress and participants.

© Bettmann/CORBIS

and the absence of federal intervention, the local movement in Albany appeared to be grounding to a halt with little to show for its efforts. To cap it all, Judge Elliot began hearings on the city's request for a permanent restraining order against any further demonstrations.

With the local movement in Albany getting increasingly bogged down, on 1 August President Kennedy appeared to offer at least a glimmer of hope. Throughout the Albany Campaign, the position of the Kennedy administration had been to prefer a local settlement without the need for its intervention. Yet the last thing the administration wanted was a protracted campaign of demonstrations and arrests without any sign of resolution. Asked about developments in the city at a press conference, Kennedy observed that the United States was currently 'involved in sitting down at Geneva with the Soviet Union. I can't understand why the government of Albany, City Council of Albany, cannot do the same for American citizens.'

King congratulated Kennedy for his comments and expressed his hope that 'you will continue to use the great moral influence of your office to help this crucial situation'. Mayor Kelley dismissed the President's comments as 'inappropriate [since] this is a purely local problem'. He added that the city would 'never negotiate with outside agitators'. King countered by offering 'to call off the marches and return to . . . Atlanta to give the commission a chance to "save face" and demonstrate good faith with the Albany Movement'. The city believed that it was in fact King who was trying to save face by fleeing a failing local movement in Albany. One city official boasted that 'firm but fair law enforcement [has] broken the back of the Albany Movement'.

The following night, various representatives of civil rights organizations, including the SCLC, CORE and the NAACP, met with Robert Kennedy and Burke Marshall in Washington DC to discuss developments in Albany. Kennedy and Marshall both indicated that the administration favoured a swift local settlement, but insisted that this could not be achieved while King remained on the scene.

Further federal intervention came on Wednesday 8 August when the Justice Department joined movement attorneys in opposition to the city's attempts to win a permanent injunction against demonstrations. On Friday 10 August, King and Abernathy were both found guilty over their 27 July arrest, but had their 60-day jail sentences and $200 fines suspended, thus paving the way for them to leave the city. After speaking at mass rallies that night, King left Albany. Over the weekend, city commissioners poured scorn on King's retreat by declaring that while they were pleased at his departure it did nothing to change their non-committal stance.

King tried several last-ditch attempts to keep the local movement in Albany alive. He returned on 27 August to offer support for two groups of white northern ministers who offered to mediate in the dispute. The city subsequently arrested 75 of the ministers for holding a prayer vigil outside City Hall. King then sent a telegram to President Kennedy asking him to assist in mediation efforts. There was no reply. Having achieved its goal of ending demonstrations, the Kennedy administration had no desire to further involve itself with the Albany Movement. The City Commission continued to hold strong against any changes to the segregated order.

The Albany Campaign had left blacks 'disillusioned, frightened and bitter', reported Albany Movement leader Slater King. Writing two years after the 1961–1962 movement, one news reporter concluded that Albany still represented a 'monument to white supremacy'. At the end of 1963, chief of police Laurie Pritchett could boast that 'Albany is as segregated as ever.' NAACP executive secretary Roy Wilkins, commenting on the Albany Movement, noted that 'Direct action, for all the exhilaration it had produced in Montgomery, with the sit-ins and the Freedom Rides, had suddenly come up against a hard, unmoving rock.' More than ever, pressure grew on King to prove that he still deserved the mantle of movement leader.

Further reading

The Albany campaign lacks its own monograph and has received the least attention of any of King and the SCLC's campaigns. It is partially covered in Pat Watters and Reese Cleghorn, *Climbing Jacob's Ladder* (1967) and Pat Watters, *Down to Now: Reflections on the Southern Civil Rights Movement* (1971). A critical analysis of King's role can be found in the article by John A. Ricks, 'De Lawd Descends and is Crucified: Martin Luther King, Jr. in Albany, Georgia', *Journal of South-West Georgia History* 2 (Fall 1984), 3–14. The wider struggle for civil rights in Georgia is outlined in Stephen G. N. Tuck, *Beyond Atlanta: The Struggle for Racial Equality in Georgia, 1940–1980* (2001).

7

The Birmingham Campaign, 1963

Although the Albany Movement ended in defeat for King and the SCLC, it proved a valuable learning experience. King and the SCLC used their experiences in Albany to reflect on the mistakes that they had made there and to devise a better-planned strategy for their next campaign in Birmingham, Alabama.

In choosing Birmingham, King and the SCLC went to a place that symbolized violent white southern racism, personified in public safety commissioner Bull Connor, who had allowed Freedom Riders to be beaten by a white mob in the city in 1961. At the same time, Birmingham's white business community was wary of the damage that its racist reputation was having on the city's image in the nation. Birmingham businessmen had already indicated a tentative willingness to introduce limited changes in racial practices. The **Alabama Christian Movement for Human Rights (ACMHR)**, under the leadership of Rev. Fred Shuttlesworth, was one of the SCLC's most active affiliates and the leading civil rights organization in the city, which King and the SCLC hoped would ensure greater unity in demonstrations.

Despite their best-laid plans, however, King and the SCLC encountered a number of difficulties in Birmingham. Political developments in the city delayed the start of the campaign. Complaints from local black leaders and white sympathizers about the use of non-violent direct action tactics threatened movement unity. Too few blacks were willing to join demonstrations. King and other SCLC staff members fast discovered that although they could target the places most conducive to successful demonstrations, no movement that involved so many different factors could ever be totally under their control.

Birmingham's black population, like Albany's, stood at around 40 per cent of the city population. Yet with a much larger total population of 350,000, the city held out the prospect of a campaign on a much larger scale. The largest centre of heavy industry in the South, Birmingham's economy was built around iron and steel production. The city held a reputation as one of the most violent and racist cities in the United States. In the post-war era,

Alabama Christian Movement for Human Rights: SCLC-affiliated civil rights organization headed by Rev. Fred Shuttlesworth.

racial violence had manifested itself in the dynamiting of black residents who attempted to move from cramped black neighbourhoods into white neighbourhoods. The violence earned the city the nickname of 'Bombingham'. King felt that Birmingham's reputation as a symbol of white violence meant that if the SCLC could 'break the back of segregation' there it could do it 'all over the nation'.

The SCLC scheduled the start of its campaign for 14 March, after local elections for a new Mayor-Council government in Birmingham. Bull Connor was running for mayor against two other candidates, former state lieutenant governor Albert Boutwell and Thomas King. Both Boutwell and Thomas King declared themselves supporters of segregation, but insisted that they disagreed with Connor's brutal policing methods.

King and the SCLC hoped that a new leadership in the city would be more open to discussion and change. However, on the day of the election there was no clear majority winner, with Boutwell narrowly ahead on 39 per cent to Connor's 31 per cent of votes. A run-off election between Boutwell and Connor was set for 2 April. The run-off forced the SCLC to 'remap strategy' and to delay the start of the campaign until 3 April.

On 2 April, Boutwell beat Connor in the run-off election by 58 per cent to 42 per cent of votes. Yet Connor refused to give way. He sued for the right to see out his original term of office as public safety commissioner that he held under the old form of city government. This in effect meant that two different administrations laid claim to govern the city. Boutwell decided to wait until the courts ruled on the matter before taking office, which left Connor still in office. Against this backdrop of political confusion, the SCLC launched its campaign on 3 April. Soon, Birmingham would have, as one local put it, 'two mayors, one King, and a parade every day'.

As King and his SCLC advisers had previously agreed, demonstrations began with small groups targeting downtown lunch counters with sit-ins. A number of arrests were made. King, meanwhile, continued to stress the importance of putting pressure on the city's white businessmen with a boycott of selected downtown stores during the busy Easter shopping period. He believed that Birmingham's large black population possessed 'significant buying power so that its withdrawal could make the difference between profit and loss for many businesses'.

No sooner had the campaign got under way than several unanticipated problems came to light. The number of local blacks willing to volunteer to participate in demonstrations was far below SCLC's expectations. In the run-up to the Birmingham campaign, Fred Shuttlesworth had downplayed just how widespread that reluctance was.

Likewise, Shuttlesworth had glossed over his rivalries with influential black middle-class leaders in the city. Those leaders now began, privately, to voice strong reservations about the timing of the SCLC's demonstrations. They insisted that the Boutwell administration should be given a chance to address the city's racial problems before SCLC demonstrations began. Local black newspaper the *Birmingham World* declared that 'direct action seems to be both wasteful and reckless'. White clergymen in the city who were sympathetic to black demands, along with the Kennedy administration, insisted that the timing of the demonstrations was inappropriate.

Whilst King defended his decision to launch the Birmingham Campaign, another problem arose. Bull Connor, aware of Laurie Pritchett's successful policing tactics in Albany, was attempting to emulate them. At Connor's request, the Ku Klux Klan violence that had long plagued the city disappeared. King admitted that he was 'surprised at the restraint of Connor's men'. Still vying for public support to remain in office, Connor insisted that he would 'fill the jail if they violate the laws as long as I am at City Hall'. However, Connor's policy of appeasement did not last long. On Sunday 9 April, King's brother, A. D. King, who was a church minister in Birmingham, led a march downtown. Connor brought out snarling police dogs to keep the marchers in line.

Watching the scene unfold, SCLC's Wyatt Walker stumbled upon an important discovery. Although the actual protest was made up of barely 20 people, the number of black onlookers it attracted gave the impression of a much larger demonstration. Viewing this as a cunning way to make up for a lack of movement volunteers, Walker planned further demonstrations at peak times of the day when they would attract more of this residual support. As it had in Albany, involving non-movement people carried with it the risk of undisciplined, even violent demonstrations. Yet in Birmingham the tactic would be vindicated to a large extent by the disproportionate counter-violence used by the police. Walker renamed the Birmingham Campaign from its initial 'Project X' to 'Project C' for confrontation.

On 8 and 9 April, King met with groups of Birmingham's black ministers and black middle-class leaders to convince them that this was the time for the movement to press home its demands. Gradually winning them around, they agreed to open negotiations with white businessmen, but made little progress. In an attempt to place pressure on the white business community to hold meaningful negotiations, King declared that he and Ralph Abernathy would lead a march on Good Friday, 12 April, and that they would face arrest and if necessary go to jail.

Already anticipating this move, the city won a state court injunction against further marches or demonstrations. The hope was that such legal action, as in Albany, would stop the movement in its tracks. This time, however, King was prepared for such a move and he was willing to accept the previous arguments made by SNCC that the movement had a duty to break unjust laws. Nevertheless, he was careful to make the distinction between defying a state court order issued by a court that upheld local and state segregation laws, as opposed to a federal court order by a court that was willing to uphold federal law and declare local and state segregation laws invalid. King declared that the march would go ahead despite the state court injunction.

King began Friday morning with a new problem. The SCLC's funds for bail money were already depleted and anyone now arrested in Birmingham could not be guaranteed release from jail. This point was crucial since, as in Albany, few local people could afford to commit to remaining in jail on an indefinite basis as they had jobs to go to and families to feed. Thus King faced a dilemma. Should he leave Birmingham to raise bail money for the movement or should he stay in Birmingham and go to jail? If he left it would look like another retreat. If he stayed he would be stuck in jail and unable to help those incarcerated alongside him. As he deliberated, King felt that he was 'standing . . . at the center of all that my life had brought me to be'.

Despite the problems that it might entail, King told his advisers that he had resolved to 'make a faith act' and to go to jail as planned. SCLC's Andrew Young later reflected that the decision marked 'the beginning of [King's] true leadership' of the movement, in that King showed himself willing to move beyond his previous cautious stance and to take more risks to provide more dynamic movement leadership.

That afternoon, King and Abernathy, clad in blue denim overalls to show their unity with Birmingham's working-class black citizenry, led 50 demonstrators on a march from Sixth Avenue Baptist Church to City Hall. After a few blocks, Connor told his men to 'Stop them. Don't let them go any farther.' Police officers arrested all of the marchers and drove them downtown to the city jail.

While incarcerated, King penned a 'Letter From Birmingham City Jail' in response to the earlier criticisms of eight prominent white Alabama clergymen about his use of non-violent direct action tactics [Doc. 11, p. 143]. The letter was one of King's most eloquent and thoughtful defences of the use of non-violence and civil disobedience, although its publication and widespread dissemination came only after the major events of the Birmingham campaign had passed.

On 22 April, King and ten other defendants were found guilty on the charge of violating the court injunction against marching or demonstrations. Each was sentenced to five days in jail and a $50 fine, which was held in abeyance on appeal. At a mass meeting on Friday evening, King again underlined the importance of the economic boycott of white-owned downtown stores and announced an expansion of demonstrations. Yet, as he left Birmingham for speaking engagements elsewhere that weekend, Wyatt Walker and James Bevel, an SCLC field secretary recruited from the student sit-in movement in

Nashville, were left in charge of operations and found it increasingly difficult to recruit movement volunteers.

Bevel noted that the most eager recruits were black high school students. When King arrived back in Birmingham on Monday 30 April, Bevel urged him to tap this student support. Bevel explained that 'A boy from high school . . . can get the same effect in terms of being in jail, in terms of putting the pressure on the city, as his father – and yet there is no economic threat on the family because the father is still in his job.'

Using children in demonstrations was a controversial move. Many black adults naturally objected to their offspring being placed in danger. Much earlier in the movement, when King had suggested encouraging the use of non-violent direct action in high schools, NAACP attorney Thurgood Marshall had stated that he did not 'approve of using children to do men's work'. Strong opposition to the tactic in Birmingham came from an array of sources. Birmingham's mayor-elect Albert Boutwell condemned the move-ment for using 'innocent children as their tools'. Robert Kennedy warned that 'An injured, maimed or dead child is a price that none of us can afford to pay.' In Harlem, Nation of Islam minister and spokesperson Malcolm X stormed that 'Real men don't put their children on the firing line.'

Recognizing just how damaging the tactic of using child demonstrators might be to the movement, and the criticism that it would draw, King was hesitant about giving an open endorsement to Bevel's plan. But while King hesitated, Bevel acted. Without King's explicit approval, Bevel began to mobilize black student support from Birmingham's high schools.

On Thursday 2 May, hundreds of young would-be demonstrators filled Sixteenth Street Baptist Church. At the same time, Connor's police forces gathered at Kelley Ingram Park near the church, on a small patch of grassland that divided a predominantly black part of the city from the white downtown. With a stand-off in the making, Bevel and Walker moved to implement what turned out to be the decisive tactical decision of the Birmingham campaign. King would later call it 'one of the wisest moves we made'.

Bevel and Walker sent a first wave of several hundred high school dem-onstrators on a march to City Hall. Birmingham police arrested the marchers. A second, then a third wave of demonstrators followed. Again, the police arrested them all. Bevel took charge of organizing the youngsters while Walker coordinated the demonstrations, communicating with SCLC staff over walkie-talkies. By that evening, over 500 arrests had been made. For the first time ever, the SCLC was actually able to hold good on its promise to fill the jails. As Bevel had predicted, with their children involved the black adult community rallied to the aid of the movement. Over 2,000 local blacks attended a mass movement that night.

The following afternoon demonstrations continued. Fast losing patience, Connor set free the police dogs and had the fire department, also under his control, train spray from high-powered hoses on demonstrators. David Vann, a white Birmingham attorney, reported that because of Connor's tactics 'in a twinkling of an eye, the whole black community was instantaneously consolidated behind King'. Moreover, the scenes of violence got the attention of the President. Although there was still no mandate for federal intervention, Kennedy admitted that the news reports and images of the police dogs attacking demonstrators had made him feel 'sick'.

Burke Marshall and Joseph Dolan, an assistant deputy attorney general, were dispatched to the city to assist in a negotiated settlement. Under pressure from federal representatives and fearing a mass outbreak of violence and disorder, white businessmen in Birmingham agreed to open negotiations with black community representatives.

Meanwhile, the movement continued to keep up the pressure in the streets. A demonstration on Friday 4 May resulted yet again in the use of high-powered fire hoses against demonstrators. Bevel, sensing an increasingly agitated and violent mood among black demonstrators, feared that he might lose control of events.

Against the backdrop of continuing demonstrations, negotiations between white businessmen and black representatives began. The white businessmen were presented with the movement's four principal demands. Firstly, downtown store facilities must desegregate. Secondly, existing black employees must be upgraded and non-discriminatory hiring practices adopted in the future. Thirdly, white businessmen must put pressure on the city government to drop charges against movement demonstrators. Fourthly, white businessmen must put pressure on the city government to form a biracial negotiating committee to conduct further discussions.

The reply was not promising. White businessmen refused to negotiate on points three and four since they insisted that they involved the city government and not them. They also insisted that no action on points one and two could be taken until the existing stalemate over who actually ran city government had been resolved in the courts. With little progress, white negotiators decided that a larger representative body was needed to encompass the scope of black demands. They therefore called upon the help of the **Senior Citizens Committee**, a group of senior white businessmen sponsored by the city's Chamber of Commerce, which had originally been formed to push through local government reform.

Senior Citizens Committee: A group of senior white businessmen that negotiated with civil rights representatives in the 1963 Birmingham Campaign.

On the afternoon of Tuesday 7 May, the Senior Citizens Committee met amid further demonstrations. From past experience in Albany, King and the SCLC knew that they needed to keep pressure on the city to make concessions while negotiations took place. The Senior Citizens Committee agreed that it had to act decisively. With only a few dissenting voices, an agreement was reached to pursue a meaningful settlement with black representatives.

On Friday morning, 10 May, King held a press conference to announce the settlement terms of the 'Birmingham Truce Agreement'. Firstly, three days after the close of demonstrations, downtown stores would desegregate their waiting rooms. Secondly, 30 days after the court order to install the Boutwell administration, segregation signs on washrooms, restrooms, and drinking fountains would be removed. Thirdly, 60 days after the court order to install the Boutwell administration, the desegregation of lunch counters would begin. Fourthly, when the court order to install the Boutwell administration was handed down a programme of black employment upgrading would begin immediately; within 60 days that programme would include at least one black sales person or cashier; and within 15 days after demonstrations ending, a biracial Committee on Racial Problems and Employment would be established.

King was at pains to emphasize that the SCLC would not repeat the mistake of Albany and simply leave after an agreement had been reached. Rather, this time, King insisted, he and the SCLC would stay to help the black community through the process of desegregation and launch a voter registration drive to consolidate existing gains and force further concessions.

On Saturday morning, 11 May, King left Birmingham to return to Atlanta. That evening, the full fury of a white backlash against the truce agreement was unleashed. For six weeks the hallmark of Ku Klux Klan violence in the city, terror bombings, had been absent. With news of the truce agreement they returned with a vengeance. The targets were A. D. King's home and M. L. King, Jr.'s vacated room at the Gaston Motel. Fortunately, no one was injured, but the blasts did bring angry black crowds out onto the streets.

Robert Kennedy feared that if violence continued in Birmingham it might also spread to other cities across the country. He dispatched two more federal assistants, Ramsey Clark and John Nolan, to the city. After consulting with Burke Marshall and King, President Kennedy decided to federalize the Alabama National Guard by bringing it under his control as Commander-in-Chief of the armed forces, to prevent its possible use by Alabama governor George Wallace, and to move federal troops close to Birmingham for reinforcements if they should be needed. That night, the President appeared on national television to inform the people of the United States about his decision to back the truce agreement in Birmingham.

The Birmingham Campaign was to King and the SCLC what the sit-ins were to SNCC and what the Freedom Rides were to CORE. Ever since the Montgomery boycott, King had struggled to find his place in the emerging civil rights movement. Now, in Birmingham, he – and the SLC – found a strategy that represented their own distinctive brand of non-violent direct action. Moreover, the success of the Birmingham Campaign inspired an upsurge in black activism in other southern communities during the summer of 1963 – a 'contagion of the will to be free', as King put it.

The essence of King and the SCLC's evolving strategy was to choose a community that they felt was conducive and susceptible to demonstrations; they would seek negotiations with the white community for change; they would engage in the short-term mobilization of the black population and train them in non-violence; and if negotiations with the white community subsequently failed, they would launch non-violent direct action demonstrations to highlight the injustices that existed in the community. In holding demonstrations, King and the SCLC hoped that they would force local whites to the negotiating table or draw violent opposition to change that would bring outside help in the form of federal intervention.

In implementing this strategy, King and the SCLC encountered a number of criticisms. SNCC decried it as insensitive, claiming that King and the SCLC exploited communities for their own ends and failed to take into account the needs of local blacks over a desire for national headlines. Moreover, SNCC claimed, King and the SCLC failed to provide the support that black communities needed after demonstrations finished that would enable them to continue the fight for civil rights after King and the SCLC left.

Though SNCC's criticisms were indeed borne out in many cases, King and the SCLC's strategy was in many ways dictated by entirely practical constraints. The SCLC simply did not have the committed cadre of student volunteers to conduct long-term community organizing campaigns that SNCC did, nor did it have the finances to pay staff members to engage in and to support such projects.

Rather, the SCLC strategy was designed to maximize its resources and play to its own particular strengths: it relied upon King's national standing to bring federal action and legislation though pressure exerted in local campaigns, in the hope and expectation that federal action and national legislation would ultimately benefit blacks in the South and in the nation as a whole. Of course, ideally, the SCLC would have wanted to provide an extensive local support network to help implement this legislation. But it could not financially afford to do so.

Whites criticized King and the SCLC's strategy by claiming that although it pretended to be non-violent, it actually provoked violence by seeking out confrontation. King responded to this criticism by noting that non-violent direct action demonstrations merely brought to the surface the latent violence that kept segregation and racial discrimination in place. He reasoned that if black demonstrators were allowed to exercise their constitutional civil rights, there would be no reason for whites to use violence to stop them from doing so in the first place.

King and the SCLC would return to the Birmingham strategy repeatedly over the following three years with mixed results, constantly seeking to evolve that strategy to address new issues and to respond to the variety of different local conditions and contexts in which it operated.

Further reading

The best study of the civil rights struggle and the SCLC campaign in Birmingham is Glenn T. Eskew, *But For Birmingham: The Local and National Movements in the Civil Rights Struggle* (1997). On influential local activist Fred Shuttlesworth see Andrew M. Mannis, *A Fire You Can't Put Out: The Civil Right's Life of Birmingham's Fred Shuttlesworth* (1999). Dianne McWhorter, *Carry Me Home: Birmingham, Alabama – The Climactic Battle of the Civil Rights Revolution* (2001) is a scholarly account written by a local white woman from a prominent family in the city. On King's 'Letter from Birmingham City Jail' see Jonathan S. Bass, *Blessed Are The Peacemakers: Martin Luther King, Jr., Eight White Religious Leaders, and the 'Letter from Birmingham City Jail'* (2001).

Part 4

KING AND AN EXPANDING MOVEMENT, 1963–1965

8

The March on Washington, 1963

The 1963 March on Washington had its origins in a similar demonstration planned by A. Philip Randolph in 1941, which he had threatened to lead if President Franklin D. Roosevelt did not act to combat racial discrimination in wartime industries. After Roosevelt met with Randolph and agreed to take action the planned march was cancelled. Roosevelt subsequently issued Executive Order 8802, which banned racial discrimination in wartime industry hiring practices, and set up the Fair Employment Practices Committee (FEPC) to enforce the ban.

On a December afternoon in 1962, at the Brotherhood of Sleeping Car Porters Union office in New York City, Randolph and Bayard Rustin discussed the idea of reprising a '**March on Washington for Jobs and Freedom**' to mark the 100th anniversary of President Abraham Lincoln's signing of the Emancipation Proclamation, and to focus attention on the ongoing problems of black employment opportunities and economic injustice.

In June 1963, plans for the March on Washington evolved into an event that promised to unite all of the major civil rights organizations in one single demonstration. Representatives of those organizations were in New York on 17 June to attend a meeting called by Taconic Foundation president Stephen R. Currier. At the meeting, Currier suggested the formation of a **Council for United Civil Rights Leadership (CUCRL)** that would collect and then distribute large financial contributions to the movement between the leading organizations to avoid squabbles over funding. Since Currier played an important role in securing such donations, the representatives of all the organizations agreed to the plan.

The following day, Currier met with King, Ralph Abernathy, Fred Shuttlesworth, Stanley Levison, Bayard Rustin and others at Randolph's office. The group agreed that a March on Washington would take place in August 1963 and they named New York black unionist Cleveland Robinson and New York pastor George Lawrence, both of whom were already involved with Randolph's plans for the march, as temporary coordinators. A meeting

March on Washington for Jobs and Freedom: One of the largest civil rights gatherings of the 1960s with around 250,000 people participating at the Lincoln Memorial and Reflecting Pool in Washington DC.

Council for United Civil Rights Leadership: Made up of the 'Big Six' civil rights organizations and formed to collect and distribute financial contributions to the civil rights movement.

was set for 24 June to discuss plans further. On 21 June, Robinson and Lawrence announced the march to the press.

News of the march brought a summons for what the press called the 'Big Six' civil rights leaders – A. Philip Randolph (president of the BSCPU), Martin Luther King, Jr. (president of the SCLC), Roy Wilkins (executive secretary of the NAACP), Whitney Young (executive director of the National Urban League), James Farmer (national director of CORE) and John Lewis (the newly elected chair of SNCC) – to the White House.

In the wake of the Birmingham demonstrations, the Kennedy administration was beginning to take a more forthright stand on civil rights. On 1 June 1963, Attorney General Robert Kennedy had met with key administration strategists to advocate legislation that would empower the federal government to be more proactive in the area. Both President Kennedy and Vice President Lyndon B. Johnson agreed, although others present protested that such legislation would be difficult to get through a Congress that included many powerful southern politicians opposed to such a measure.

Yet precisely the need for such legislation was evident on 11 June when Alabama governor George Wallace stood in the doorway of the University of Alabama, Tuscaloosa, and physically barred the entrance of Deputy Attorney General Nicholas Katzenbach and two black students who were attempting to enrol there under federal court order. President Kennedy federalized the Alabama National Guard to enforce the law and the students were eventually admitted.

That same night, in a separate incident, Mississippi NAACP leader Medgar Evers was shot dead in the drive of his home by white segregationist Byron De La Beckwith. President Kennedy appeared on national television to deliver his strongest speech yet in support of civil rights, telling the audience that 'We are confronted primarily with a moral issue' which was 'as old as the scriptures and is as clear as the American Constitution'. Kennedy announced that a civil rights bill would be introduced to Congress and that it would contain a provision requiring the desegregation of all public facilities and accommodations.

When Kennedy met with civil rights leaders on 22 June he was concerned that the proposed March on Washington might hinder rather than help the already expected difficult passage of the civil rights bill through Congress. The President told them, 'We want success in Congress not just a big show at the capital. Some of these people [in Congress] are looking for an excuse to be against us. I don't want to give them a chance to say "Yes, I'm for the bill, but I'm damned if I'll vote for it at the point of a gun."' Both King and James Farmer resolutely defended the march and insisted that it would go ahead as planned.

King, undoubtedly with Kennedy's words partly in mind, later dismissed the 'prophets of doom who feared that the slightest incidence of violence would alienate Congress and destroy all hope of legislation'. A. Philip Randolph was also adamant that the march would take place, telling Kennedy, 'The Negroes are already in the streets. If they are bound to be in the streets in any case is it not better that they be led by organizations dedicated to civil rights and disciplined by struggle rather than to leave them to other leaders who care neither about civil rights or nonviolence?'

Randolph's mention of 'other leaders' who did not care about 'civil rights or nonviolence' was clearly a reference to the growing popularity of the **Black Muslim** sect the Nation of Islam (NOI) and in particular its charismatic spokesperson Malcolm X. A fiery, controversial and provocative speaker (SCLC's Wyatt Walker almost got into a fistfight with him when they debated on one television show), Malcolm X was the most visible and vocal critic of King, of non-violence, and of white America [**Doc. 12, p. 143**].

> **Black Muslims:** An umbrella term for organizations promoting the interests of black Muslims, the most well known being the Nation of Islam.

Malcolm X was born Malcolm Little in Omaha, Nebraska, in 1925. His life was shaped by his experiences in the northern ghetto. His father died in a streetcar accident when Malcolm was only six years old and his mother was committed to a mental institution eight years later, leaving him to be raised in a juvenile home, then with foster parents, and then with his half-sister Ella in Boston. Like many black ghetto youths with scant opportunities in a white-dominated society, Malcolm drifted into a life of drugs and crime. While in jail after an arrest for burglary Malcolm Little underwent a religious conversion to Islam and dropped his 'slave name' for an 'X' to signify his unknown African ancestry.

Taken under the wing of NOI leader Elijah Muhammad, Malcolm fast became the organization's most effective proponent. Malcolm's speeches espoused NOI dogma, calling whites 'snakes' and 'devils', which struck a resonant chord among many alienated black northern youth and provided a form of psychological release from white oppression. So, too, did Malcolm's stress on race pride, his encouragement of his followers to explore their African identity, and his advocacy of resistance to whites 'by any means necessary', including the use of **armed self-defence** and outright violence.

> **Armed Self-Defence:** Taking up weapons to prevent being attacked.

In many ways, Malcolm X was a figure that linked earlier black nationalist and black separatist leaders and organizations, such as Marcus Garvey and the Universal Negro Improvement Association (UNIA), of which Malcolm's father had been a member, to the later development of Black Power. As with Garvey, the UNIA and Black Power, however, Malcolm X often stood accused by critics of lacking a plausible programme for converting a feeling of black psychological empowerment into actual social, political and economic power for the black community.

Malcolm X was (and remains) a figure that represented the very antithesis of King in the minds of many blacks and whites, although in later years, after a break with the NOI in the winter of 1963–1964, he began to moderate his views and rhetoric somewhat. What direction Malcolm X might have eventually taken will never be known: in February 1965 members of the NOI assassinated him. During Malcolm X's lifetime, King and other movement leaders often exploited his angry and incendiary rhetoric to their advantage, since they were able to point to Malcolm and the NOI's stance as the alternative that whites faced if they refused the civil rights movement's more moderate and reasonable demands.

At the 24 June meeting to discuss plans for the March on Washington, to placate anxious leaders like the NAACP's Roy Wilkins who was worried about calls for the march to employ mass civil disobedience, Randolph offered the assurance that the main focus of the demonstration would be a one-day non-violent march held on Wednesday 28 August. Although SNCC was not pleased at the watered-down plan, Randolph's assurance did persuade Wilkins to grudgingly give NAACP backing to the march.

At the follow-up meeting on 2 July, Rustin put forward more detailed plans. Reflecting the original idea of Randolph and Rustin, economic issues, such as demands for better jobs for blacks and a higher minimum wage, were prioritized. Passage of the civil rights bill was listed only as a secondary concern. The Big Six leaders would serve as co-chairs of the march, with each appointing a fellow member of their respective organizations as administrative coordinators. Randolph was nominated as march director and chose Rustin to be his deputy.

As preparations got under way, plans for a more restrained demonstration pleased those who had initially worried that it would lead to a full-scale repeat of the Birmingham Campaign. Even President Kennedy endorsed the march at a 17 July press conference.

United Auto Workers: Labour union representing auto workers and one of the strongest labour movement supporters of civil rights.

In early August, Randolph announced four white co-chairs of the march: **United Auto Workers'** president Walter Reuther and three white religious leaders from Protestant, Catholic and Jewish faiths. The new appointments emphasized the biracial and interfaith nature of the march and broadened the movement's base of support. The committee intended to seek an audience with President Kennedy after the completion of the march and the planned afternoon speeches.

King arrived late in Washington on Tuesday 27 August, the day before the scheduled march, and missed the deadline for speakers to hand in advance texts of their speeches to the press. He hurriedly sketched out his remarks for distribution the following morning.

It was not the text of King's speech, however, but that of SNCC's John Lewis that was causing most concern on Wednesday morning. Lewis's controversial and incendiary tract criticized the Kennedy administration for doing 'too little and too late' in the field of civil rights. Lewis wrote of the violence being endured by civil rights workers in the South, the ongoing denial of black voting rights, and the economic plight of the black community, while condemning 'cheap political leaders who build their careers on immoral compromises'. Lewis also spoke of the 'revolution' taking place in America's streets and threatened to 'burn Jim Crow to the ground', metaphorically emulating the 'scorched earth' policy of Republican Civil War General William T. Sherman.

Robert Kennedy and Burke Marshall were not at all happy with the text of Lewis's speech. They used Cardinal Patrick O'Boyle, the Washington DC Catholic priest who was due to deliver the invocation at the march, to exert pressure on its leaders. O'Boyle threatened to withdraw from proceedings if Lewis did not change the tone of his speech.

Rustin went to Lewis's hotel room to plead the case for changing the text in the interests of harmony, but Lewis was unrepentant. The controversy over Lewis's text was still raging as the march leaders gathered at the Lincoln Memorial. Eventually, Randolph persuaded a reluctant Lewis to deliver a revised version of his speech. Two Kennedy aides stood by the speakers ready to silence Lewis by literally pulling the plug if he reneged on his agreement.

In the event, it was King's 'I Have A Dream' speech that most people would remember. Some had criticized Rustin for putting King on as the last speaker. But, Rustin remembered, 'almost all the other speakers had asked me to make sure they didn't follow King. They knew that King was the key figure at that time in the civil rights history; and they realized the minute King finished speaking the program would be over, that everybody would be heading home.'

On a hot balmy August afternoon, King began with his prepared text but towards the end, responding to the emotional intensity of the occasion, he went to an improvised finale. King laid bare his vision of an integrated South with a repetition of paragraphs beginning with 'I have a dream'. Then, in a final flourish, he seized upon the peroration 'Let Freedom Ring' to bring his speech to a crescendo that brought thunderous applause from the audience.

Of course, King's preaching style and rhetoric was nothing new to those who knew him well, and his spontaneous break from the prepared text essentially repeated the content of earlier speeches made in Birmingham and Detroit in April and June that year. However, to those millions who watched either the live broadcast or later reruns on television, many of whom were white and who had never heard or seen a southern black Baptist preacher deliver a sermon before, King's performance was a new and electrifying experience that made the speech's emotional impact even greater and framed the sense of occasion even more poignantly. This ensured that of all the events that took place that day, King's speech has remained the point of focus in the nation's collective memory.

Different people from different constituencies of the movement remember and interpret King's 'I Have A Dream' speech in different ways. To Fred Shuttlesworth, King's words were nothing short of divine intervention.

'There are good words said every day,' Shuttlesworth noted, 'But every once in a while, God intervenes in such a way that you know only God could do it. That was God preaching the Gospel to America through King. It helped to change the mind-set of America.'

Ralph Abernathy viewed the speech as a commanding oratorical performance – 'one of those few public utterances that inevitably becomes a part of the oral tradition of a people, never to be forgotten'. SCLC's Andrew Young saw King's speech and the March on Washington in terms of movement politics, remembering that 'The march transformed what had been a southern movement into a national movement.'

Others felt that King's speech revealed ongoing problems with his leadership. Mississippi activist Anne Moody was disappointed that 'we had "dreamers" instead of leaders leading us . . . in Canton [Mississippi] we never had time to sleep, much less dream'. Even while King enjoyed one of his finest hours on the public stage, throughout his speech a black heckler at the front of the crowd urged greater black militancy, screaming 'Fuck that dream, Martin. Now, goddamnit, NOW!'

In contrast to the prominence that is now often accorded to the March on Washington in the popular memory of the civil rights movement, many assessments at the time questioned exactly what the march had achieved. The *New York Times* reported that the march 'appeared to have left much of Congress untouched – physically, emotionally, and politically'. Lerone Bennett, Jr., senior editor of *Ebony* magazine and a contemporary of King's at Morehouse College, noted that the march 'led nowhere and it was not intended to lead anywhere. It was not planned as an event within a coherent plan of action.' Malcolm X dismissed the whole thing as a 'Farce on Washington'.

Federal Bureau of Investigation: The United States' federal criminal investigation and intelligence agency.

The **FBI** was far more impressed. As a result of the march, the bureau labelled King the 'most dangerous and effective Negro leader in the country'. Within three months it had persuaded Robert Kennedy to give the order that allowed it to start wiretapping King's home phone and SCLC offices in Atlanta and New York. Later, without even bothering to seek permission first, they extended surveillance to King's hotel rooms.

Although the direct political impact of the March on Washington on the President and Congress admittedly proved negligible, as a public relations showcase for the movement it more than fulfilled its purpose. As Ralph Abernathy perceptively later noted: 'Ceremonies of this sort have an important effect on the consciousness of a community or a people, even if they don't result in concrete actions.'

Around 200,000 people had packed the area between the Lincoln Memorial and the Washington Monument around the reflecting pool at the heart of the nation's capital, giving at least the appearance of a united and determined movement with mass support. Importantly, thanks largely to Bayard Rustin's meticulous preparations and organizational efficiency, the march passed off without any violence and emphasized the discipline and self-control of the demonstrators. This underlined the movement's contention that it was white oppression and not black activism that had led to unrest in previous civil rights campaigns.

The interracial element of the march was also significant, with whites accounting for around a quarter of all those present. This demonstrated to the nation that the movement did not simply represent the special interests of one section of America, but rather that it had broad-based support. In particular, the involvement of white clergymen from different faiths emphasized the moral dimensions of the struggle. For King, the 'I Have A Dream' speech confirmed his status as the leading black spokesperson in the nation.

Bayard Rustin, the most important figure in organizing the march, summed up the event by noting that, 'The march made Americans feel for the first time that we were capable of being truly a nation, that we were capable of moving beyond division and bigotry.' Being a seasoned activist, Rustin was also aware that, 'The human spirit is like a flame. It flashes up and is gone. And you never know when that flame will come again.'

Sure enough, the euphoria of the march soon gave way to tragedy. On 15 September, Sixteenth Street Baptist Church in Birmingham was hit by a dynamite blast. Four young black girls, Addie Mae Collins, Denise McNair, Carole Robertson and Cynthia Wesley, who had been attending a Sunday school service, were killed. The city exploded with violence as angry blacks confronted the police. The following morning, King demanded federal intervention to protect the black community from further white terrorism. He later delivered a moving eulogy at the funeral of three of the four girls in which he referred to them all as 'the martyred heroines of a holy crusade for freedom and dignity'.

On 22 November, President Kennedy was assassinated in Dallas, Texas. King watched the unfolding events on his television screen at home with his wife Coretta. 'This is what is going to happen to me,' King told her. 'I keep telling you, this is such a sick society.' The escalating violence and the prospect of dealing with a new president, Lyndon B. Johnson, who, as vice president, succeeded Kennedy, raised uncertainty about the future course of the civil rights movement as it entered 1964.

Further reading

On the 1963 March on Washington see Lucy G. Barber, *Marching on Washington: The Forging of an American Political Tradition* (2003); Patrick Henry Bass, *Like a Mighty Stream: The March on Washington, August 28,*

1963 (2002); Charles Euchner, *Nobody Turn Me Around: A People's History of the 1963 March on Washington* (2010); and Thomas Gentile, *March on Washington, August 28, 1963* (1983). On King's much-celebrated 'I Have a Dream' speech see Drew D. Hansen, *The Dream: Martin Luther King, Jr. and the Speech that Inspired a Nation* (2003) and Eric Sundquist, *King's Dream* (2008).

Several of the 'Big Six' movement leaders have written their own account of events: CORE's James Farmer, *Lay Bare the Heart: An Autobiography of the Civil Rights Movement* (1985); SNCC's John Lewis, *Walking With the Wind: A Memoir of the Movement* (1998); and the NAACP's Roy Wilkins, *Standing Fast: The Autobiography of Roy Wilkins* (1982). For those without first-hand accounts, there are biographies. On the NUL's Whitney Young see Dennis C. Dickerson, *Militant Mediator: Whitney M. Young, Jr.* (1998) and Nancy J. Weiss, *Whitney M. Young, Jr. and the Struggle For Civil Rights* (1989). On the BSCPU's A. Philip Randolph see Jervis Anderson, *A. Philip Randolph: A Biographical Portrait* (1973); Cornelius L. Bynum, *A. Philip Randolph and the Struggle for Civil Rights* (2010); and Paula F. Pfeffer, *A. Philip Randolph: Pioneer of the Civil Rights Movement* (1990).

Malcolm X's autobiography, as told to Alex Haley in *The Autobiography of Malcolm X* (1965) is a classic account. Manning Marable, *Malcolm X: A Life of Reinvention* (2011) is the most recent, comprehensive and controversial of the biographies. James H. Cone, *Martin, Malcolm and America: A Dream or Nightmare?* (1991) is a comparative study of the two black leaders.

9

Mississippi Freedom Summer, the MFDP and the FBI, 1964

During the first half of 1964, King and the SCLC focused on another community-based campaign in St Augustine, Florida, America's oldest city. They hoped that as the tourist-oriented city geared up for its quadricentennial celebrations in 1965, demonstrations would place pressure on local businessmen to act to avoid negative headlines. The campaign also sought to persuade Congress to pass the 1964 Civil Rights Act that President Kennedy had introduced as a bill the year before. Neither goal was successful. On the ground in St Augustine the campaign produced few tangible results. Its impact on Congress was negligible.

But the Civil Rights Act did pass in July 1964, largely thanks to the political skills of new president, Lyndon B. Johnson. Johnson, a former majority leader in the Senate, knew the processes and people in Congress well. As a Texan, he was friends with and close to many of the southern congressmen that opposed civil rights legislation. Using his political acumen and personal contacts, and presenting the civil rights act as a memorial to slain former president John F. Kennedy (even though Johnson had had a notoriously strained relationship with the Kennedy brothers), Johnson forced through the legislation.

On 2 July, King attended the signing ceremony of the 1964 Civil Rights Act that contained, among other provisions, a clause providing for the desegregation of public facilities and accommodations [**Doc. 13, p. 144**]. Though civil rights organizations geared up for a widespread testing of the act, many places took the opportunity to quietly desegregate rather than face disruption. To be sure, there were still pockets of resistance, but on a much smaller scale than anyone had initially anticipated. There seemed finally in the South to be a general resignation to the inevitable.

That did not mean that all white resistance had disappeared. With one of its major goals of desegregation secured, the movement next turned its attention to voting rights. Amendment Twenty-Four to the US Constitution, which forbade the use of the poll tax or other forms of tax as a prerequisite to voting, had been ratified in January 1964. This removed a significant barrier to black votes in a number of states. Civil rights groups now began to focus their attention on mobilizing the black franchise and building black political power.

One of the most important civil rights initiatives during the 1964 presidential election year was '**Freedom Summer**' in Mississippi. While King and the SCLC concentrated on launching a voter campaign in Alabama, SNCC, the dominant organization in the **Council of Federated Organizations (COFO)** coordinating the Mississippi Campaign, concentrated its field staff in the state and were joined by an influx of white student volunteers from northern colleges to embark upon a massive voter education and voter registration campaign.

Freedom Summer: A large-scale voter registration drive held in Mississippi in 1964.

Council of Federated Organizations: A coalition of organizations that joined together to run the 1964 Mississippi Freedom Summer.

As historians John Dittmer and Charles Payne have noted, in doing so SNCC built upon a long and rich indigenous tradition of civil rights activism and community organizing in the state. Many people in the movement saw Mississippi as the epitome of white supremacy in the South and SNCC encountered violent opposition in its efforts to build black political power in the state.

Freedom Summer captured national headlines in June 1964 when three young civil rights workers – two white New Yorkers, Michael Schwerner and Andrew Goodman, and black Mississippian James Chaney – disappeared. The discovery of their burnt-out car in a Mississippi swamp confirmed the movement's worst fears that the three men had been murdered.

As President Johnson ordered an FBI investigation of events, SNCC looked to create a **Mississippi Freedom Democratic Party (MFDP)**. SNCC insisted that the regular Mississippi Democratic Party was illegitimate because of electoral corruption in the state, which included the widespread denial of black voting rights. To offer an alternative to the 'regulars', SNCC held its own, more inclusive, 'Freedom Vote', to elect an MFDP slate of delegates to attend the 1964 Democratic National Convention.

Mississippi Freedom Democratic Party: A product of Freedom Summer, the MFDP demanded seats at the 1964 Democratic National Convention instead of the regular all-white delegation.

On 21 July, King began a five-day tour of Mississippi in a show of support for SNCC's efforts there. Threats against King's life hung over his visit. Though such threats were ever-present, they were taken seriously enough in Mississippi for President Johnson to order personal FBI protection for King while he was there. King called Freedom Summer 'one of the most creative attempts I had seen to radically challenge the oppressive life of the Negro'.

The next step in the campaign was to seat the MFDP delegation at the Democratic National Convention in Atlantic City, New Jersey. This would mean getting the delegation recognized as the legitimate Mississippi representatives at the convention and allowing them to take their seats and cast their votes for the presidential nominee. Just before the convention, on 20 August 1964, Congress passed the **Economic Opportunity Act (EOA)**, the

Economic Opportunity Act: The 1964 EOA was central to President Lyndon B. Johnson's Great Society and created a number of social programmes.

centrepiece of President Johnson's planned **War On Poverty** and an integral part of the President's desire to create a **Great Society** in the United States. Building upon and extending the programmes already initiated by the Kennedy administration to tackle poverty, the EOA, passed in the face of stiff Republican opposition, created the **Office of Economic Opportunity (OEO)** to coordinate various local and state anti-poverty programmes in areas such as social services, health services, education and employment.

The anti-poverty programmes were required to promote 'maximum feasible participation' by the poor, a term that appeared to borrow much from SNCC's grassroots organizing philosophy. The programmes proved highly controversial in terms of the amount of money spent on them, their administration and their overall effectiveness. Yet clearly, given the problems of poverty that disproportionately affected blacks in the United States, the federally funded programmes held out at least the promise of a better life and raised black expectations.

Ultimately, however, the War on Poverty would only fuel black frustration and anger when anti-poverty programmes proved to be chronically underfunded, in part because of the escalating cost of fighting the Vietnam War (see Chapter 13). Despite its eventual shortcomings, the passage of the EOA confirmed that Johnson was a socially progressive president. He was certainly preferable to the Republican presidential nominee that year, Barry Goldwater, the right-wing Arizona senator who had voted against the 1964 Civil Rights Act and was preparing for an election battle against Johnson on an anti-civil rights platform.

Conservative opposition to the EOA in Congress underlined just how politically divisive passing such legislation could be. As a wily politician, Johnson understood the need to cultivate enough conservative support to win re-election in order to push his legislative programme through Congress. It was within this conflicted political context that the 1964 Democratic National Convention unfolded.

The MFDP challenge to be seated at the convention instead of the regular Mississippi Democratic Party delegation began when the **Democratic Party Credentials Committee** held a hearing on Saturday 22 August. The MFDP's 64 delegates, four of them white, included, one observer noted, a representative sample of 'black, white, maids, ministers, carpenters, farmers, painters, mechanics, schoolteachers, the young, [and] the old' in Mississippi.

In front of the Credentials Committee, MFDP leaders, their white Washington DC attorney Joseph L. Rauh, Jr., and King, all argued for the seating of the MFDP delegation in the face of the discriminatory practices that had allowed the regular all-white state delegation to be elected. King told the Credentials Committee: 'If you value the future of democratic government, you have no alternative but to recognize, with full voice and vote, the [MFDP].'

War on Poverty: The collective term for a number of social programmes set in place by President Lyndon B. Johnson to improve the conditions of marginalized groups in American society.

Great Society: The goal of a number of social programmes set in place by President Lyndon B. Johnson to improve the condition of marginalized groups in American society.

Office of Economic Opportunity: Federal agency responsible for administering President Lyndon B. Johnson's Great Society programmes.

Democratic Party Credentials Committee: The committee charged with approving the credentials of all persons appointed or elected to the Democratic National Convention.

MFDP delegate Fannie Lou Hamer gave an emotional account of the brutalities taking place against blacks in Mississippi that was broadcast live to the nation on television. She asked the Credentials Committee, 'Is this America, the land of the free and the home of the brave, where we have to sleep with our telephones off the hooks because our lives are threatened daily, because we want to live as decent human beings, in America?' [Doc. 14, p. 146]. The Johnson administration hastily arranged a televised presidential press conference to push Hamer's powerful testimony off the airwaves.

On Sunday 23 August, Oregon Congresswoman Edith Green proposed a solution to the impasse by offering to seat any member of either of Mississippi's two delegations if they first swore a loyalty oath to the Democratic Party and its presidential ticket. The proposal highlighted the glaring irony of the situation. The MFDP delegates were all able to accept these terms since they supported Johnson, as a civil rights advocate, to stand against Republican Goldwater in the general election.

However, none of the all-white Mississippi delegation could accept these terms since they supported Goldwater and his opposition to civil rights and they were fully prepared to back the Republican candidate in the general election. Such were the convoluted politics involved that Johnson still believed that seating the MFDP delegates would be too clear a sign of his support for civil rights, which would boost Goldwater's anti-civil rights appeal and risk alienating southern Democratic congressmen and white southern voters.

The MFDP needed the votes of 11 Credentials Committee members to take their case to a vote before the whole convention. Pro-MFDP forces campaigned to win these crucial votes while Johnson's aides tried to swing committee members around to their way of thinking. As Johnson's people worked at undermining the Green proposal, they approached the MFDP with a compromise of their own: they would seat two out of the 64 MFDP delegates and give them 'at large' convention votes. That is, the two would be allowed to vote at the convention, but not as Mississippi delegates. The rest of the MFDP delegates would be seated as guests of the convention but would not be allowed to cast votes. Moreover, only those in the all-white delegation who took a loyalty oath would be allowed to cast their votes. The Democratic Party would undertake to eliminate all discrimination in delegate selection procedures by the 1968 Democratic National Convention.

Although the MFDP delegation refused to accept the compromise and continued to lobby for the preferred Green proposal, it was Johnson's plan that the Credentials Committee voted through over the protests of the MFDP and their attorney. The outcome of the vote narrowed the MFDP's options considerably. There was now only one decision. They could either accept the two-seat compromise offered by Johnson or withdraw from the convention altogether.

King was placed in a difficult situation on Tuesday 25 August, when he discussed events with other civil rights leaders and activists. Reflecting on the hard-learned lessons of the past about the need for compromise, many in the SCLC were ready to counsel the MFDP to accept the Johnson proposal as a victory, even though it by no means granted everything that the MFDP had set out to achieve. MFDP delegates opposed any compromise on the grounds that they would be betraying the ideals of all those who had worked for, voted for, and in some cases even given their lives for, the MFDP cause.

King was torn between the arguments of political pragmatism that as a national leader he fully understood and the political idealism of grassroots activists that he also strongly empathized with. King awkwardly told MFDP leaders that as a national black leader he wanted them to accept the compromise, 'but if I were a Mississippi Negro, I would vote against it'. He left the final decision to MFDP delegates.

In the heated and emotional debate that followed, movement divisions between national leaders with national goals and local leaders who were committed to fighting for change in their own communities were laid bare. The debate also brought to the fore class divisions in a movement with a largely black middle-class national leadership and a largely black working-class grassroots constituency.

As usual, the most blunt of all the national leaders was the NAACP's Roy Wilkins, who told MFDP delegates, 'You all are ignorant. You have put your point across. You should just pack your bags up and go home.' Fannie Lou Hamer, speaking for the Mississippi grassroots membership, criticized black middle-class leaders like Wilkins, declaring, 'Give 'em two dollars and a car and they think they're fine . . . [but] we didn't come all the way up here to compromise for no more than we'd gotten here . . . We didn't come all this way for two seats.'

One of the things that rankled the MFDP was the fact that the Johnson proposal dictated very specific terms. It insisted that the MFDP could have just two delegates seated and it explicitly named those two delegates: black MFDP chair Aaron Henry and white college chaplain Edwin King. In an effort to modify this proposal, and to stamp some authority on proceedings, MFDP leaders, along with King and Andrew Young of the SCLC, met with potential vice-presidential nominee Hubert Humphrey and United Auto Workers' president Walter Reuther to discuss alternative arrangements.

Two proposals emerged. One was seating all 64 delegates and then giving each of them a fraction of a vote. The other was seating four delegates with half a vote each. Hubert Humphrey warned Rustin that in light of Fannie Lou Hamer's earlier impassioned speech, under no circumstances would 'the President . . . allow that illiterate woman to speak from the floor of the convention'. With discussions still ongoing, the Democratic National Convention chair, Rhode Island senator John Pastore, appeared on the television screen that was broadcasting events live from the convention floor. In a *fait accompli*, Pastore falsely announced that the MFDP had already accepted Johnson's proposed two-vote compromise.

Johnson's duplicity enraged the MFDP delegates, who the following day voted to reject the two-seat compromise and left Atlantic City. That evening, Johnson received his party's nomination to stand for the presidency and Hubert Humphrey was selected as the party's nominee for vice president.

For SNCC, the events of the convention left a bitter aftertaste. Having worked through legitimate democratic channels to make their voices heard, only to then have their efforts undermined by political skullduggery, marked the final disillusionment with 'the system' for many in the organization. Ella Baker, who had been in Atlantic City with the MFDP delegation, recalls that events 'settled any debate [about] the possibility of functioning through the mainstream of the Democratic Party'.

Many activists felt that the movement's white liberal supporters in the Democratic Party had betrayed them. Equally, they felt betrayed by national black leaders and particularly by King in his failure to strongly back their demands. A number of commentators have pointed to the episode as a turning point in SNCC's disillusionment with mainstream politics and subsequent radicalization, which led to its later embrace of Black Power.

Yet the MFDP's efforts turned out to be more of a victory than was apparent at the time. If the MFDP did not get to take their seats at the convention, then neither did the all-white Mississippi regulars, who refused to take the required loyalty oath and also walked out of the convention. At the 1968 Democratic National Convention, the Democratic Party kept its promise to instigate reform and barred the all-white regular delegation in favour of seating MFDP delegates.

King's activities in the following months underscored the distance between himself and the rank and file of the movement. As a downtrodden SNCC and MFDP headed back to Mississippi to pick up the pieces of the struggle there, King toured Europe with his wife Coretta and Ralph Abernathy, meeting with Berlin mayor Willy Brandt and attending a personal audience with Pope Paul VI in Rome. In October, King was awarded the 1964 **Nobel Peace Prize** receiving it in December in the Norwegian capital of Oslo.

Nobel Peace Prize: One of five distinguished Nobel Prizes awarded each year by the Norwegian Nobel Committee and won by Martin Luther King, Jr. in 1965.

Despite these high-profile engagements, King was at pains to avoid self-aggrandizement. His tour was designed to publicize and to benefit the movement as a whole. He accepted the Nobel Prize on behalf of the movement's collective achievements and he donated all of the prize money that came with it back to the cause. But although King was part of the same movement as SNCC and the MFDP, his activities took him into a very different world where the rewards and glamour appeared far more tangible than the day-to-day struggle at the local level. Under these circumstances, it was difficult for many to believe that he could any longer truly identify with the civil rights movement at the grassroots level.

This impression was only reinforced when King returned from his tour to campaign in the 1964 presidential election, for Lyndon Johnson, the very man who many black activists believed had betrayed the movement in Atlantic City. Nevertheless, King rightly believed that Johnson's candidacy was far more appealing than the outright hostility to civil rights demonstrated by Republican presidential candidate Barry Goldwater. On 3 November, Johnson was returned to office with a landslide victory. King and the SCLC were determined to make sure that the newly elected president would now carry through on his promise of movement support.

If one arm of the federal bureaucracy promised to be more friendly towards the movement, then another, the FBI, proved distinctly less so. Hard on the heels of the 1964 presidential election, King found himself at the centre of a heated controversy with FBI director J. Edgar Hoover. On 18 November, Hoover labelled King 'the most notorious liar in the country' in an interview with women journalists. Hoover cited complaints from King over the FBI's conduct in Albany as the reason for his comments. However, Hoover's off-the-record utterance afterwards, that King was 'one of the lowest characters in the country', revealed a much more deep-seated personal dislike of King. As early as 1962, Hoover had made up his mind that 'King is no good.'

King replied to Hoover's comments at the press conference with a telegram that attempted to kill Hoover's comments with kindness while defending King's own earlier comments. King said he believed that Hoover must have been 'under extreme pressure' to make such a statement and expressed 'nothing but sympathy for this man who has served his country so well'. Nevertheless, King pointed to the numerous shortcomings of the FBI's civil rights record that seemed more than ample justification for any past complaints. In private, FBI wiretaps picked up King's true feelings that Hoover was getting 'old and senile' and that he should be 'hit from all sides' by a SCLC publicity counter-offensive.

In a meeting with President Johnson the day after the story broke, all of the other major civil rights leaders defended King against Hoover's accusations. This did not prevent Hoover, at a speech on 22 November, at Loyola University in Chicago, referring to certain 'pressure groups' headed by 'Communists and moral degenerates'.

King's closest advisers were divided about how to respond to Hoover's attack. Some counselled a forceful counter-attack while others cautioned King about the potential for a public battle with Hoover to do more harm than good. King eventually set up a meeting with Hoover to discuss their differences face to face. With the help of Acting Attorney General Nicholas

Katzenbach (Robert Kennedy had vacated the post to run for a US Senate seat in New York), a meeting was arranged. On 31 October, Andrew Young, Ralph Abernathy, and Walter Fauntroy, a Washington DC pastor who often served as SCLC's contact in the city, accompanied King to the meeting. Given the circumstances surrounding it, the meeting proved quite amicable.

King started the meeting on a conciliatory note, stating that many of his reported criticisms of the FBI in the press were false and that he acknowledged the importance of having a good working relationship with Hoover and his agents. Hoover's response was an almost hour-long ('You know, he talks a hell of a lot, J. Edgar Hoover,' Robert Kennedy once noted) rambling account of all of the FBI's efforts on behalf of the movement. King interjected only once to inform Hoover of the SCLC's planned campaign in Selma, Alabama, scheduled for the beginning of 1965.

The meeting ended with an agreement on both sides not to reveal the contents of their discussion to news reporters. However, the pleasantries achieved very little since they failed to address the core disagreements between the two men. Neither did the meeting bring any let-up in the efforts of the FBI to besmirch King's name. Indeed, even as the two men spoke the FBI had already hatched its most devious plot yet against King.

On 2 November, FBI assistant director William C. Sullivan ordered a taped compilation of the 'highlights' of the bureau's covert surveillance of King's hotel rooms, which allegedly contained 'dirty jokes and bawdy remarks . . . plus the sound of people [presumably including King] engaging in sex' to be sent to SCLC headquarters. The package contained a note which invited King to 'look into your heart. You know you are a complete fraud and a great liability to all of us Negroes' (Sullivan was white), and ended with a thinly veiled threat to make the tape's revelations public if King did not commit suicide or withdraw from public life before Christmas [**Doc. 15, p. 148**].

The tape did not have its intended effect of cancelling planned demonstrations in Selma. Due to the poor internal postal management system at the SCLC, the parcel was not opened until after the Selma Campaign was already under way. In fact, it was King's wife Coretta who discovered its contents when it finally turned up at their family home in Atlanta on 4 January 1965. Neither Coretta, who later dismissed the tape as 'just a lot of mumbo jumbo', nor friends pressed King on the tape's contents. Still, the tape succeeded in rattling King who confided to a friend that he believed the FBI were 'out to get me, harass me, break my spirit'.

Further reading

The local and national dimensions of King and the SCLC's 1964 St Augustine, Florida, campaign are explored in David R. Colburn, *Racial Change and*

Community Crisis: St. Augustine, Florida, 1877–1980 (1985). On the Civil Rights Act of 1964 see Hugh D. Graham, *The Civil Rights Era: Origins and Development of National Policy, 1960–1972* (1990); Robert D. Loevy, *To End All Segregation: The Politics of the Passage of the Civil Rights Act of 1964* (1990); and Charles W. Whalen and Barbara Whalen, *The Longest Debate: A Legislative History of the 1964 Civil Rights Act* (1985).

More has been written about the Mississippi Freedom Summer than any other event in the civil rights movement. Two good starting points for scholarly studies that locate Freedom Summer within the wider black organizing tradition in Mississippi are John Dittmer, *Local People: The Struggle for Civil Rights in Mississippi* (1994) and Charles Payne, *I've Got the Light of Freedom: The Organizing Tradition and the Mississippi Freedom Struggle* (1995). The classic black first-hand account of Freedom Summer is Anne Moody, *Coming of Age in Mississippi* (1968). White perspectives on Freedom Summer include Sally Belfrage, *Freedom Summer* (1965) and Mary King, *Freedom Song: A Personal Story of the 1960s Civil Rights Movement* (1987). On the 1964 murders see Seth Cagin and Philip Dray, *We Are Not Afraid: The Story of Goodman, Schwerner and Chaney and the Civil Rights Campaign for Mississippi* (1988).

Historian David Garrow has collected and edited the material gathered from FBI wiretaps on King that consists of 17,000 pages on 16 reels of microfilm. His book, David J. Garrow, *The FBI and Martin Luther King, Jr.: From 'Solo' to Memphis* (1981), analyses the FBI campaign against King using this and other material. On the harassment of the movement by the FBI more broadly see Kenneth O'Reilly, *Racial Matters: The FBI's Secret File on Black America, 1960–1972* (1989).

10

The Selma Campaign and the Voting Rights Act, 1965

S elma, Alabama, was a glaring example of the South's ongoing wide-spread denial of black voting rights. Whites accounted for 99 per cent of the electorate in Selma although they made up only approximately half of the city's 28,500 population. Complicated forms and tests were used to prevent black voter registration. Moreover, registration took place on only two days of the week. White election officials administered the whole process with extreme racial bias. Outside of Selma, in adjacent counties such as Lowndes and Wilcox, the situation was even worse. There, blacks outnumbered whites two-to-one, but not one single black person was registered to vote.

Beginning in February 1963 SNCC, in conjunction with long-standing local civil rights organizations such as the **Dallas County Voters League** (the county in which Selma was located) and the more recently founded Dallas County Improvement Association, had organized two 'Freedom Days' to register black voters. These efforts had met with resistance. Police arrested prospective black voters on a variety of charges and State Circuit judge James A. Hare issued an injunction against the local movement that virtually halted all forms of civil rights activism.

Dallas County Voters League: Local civic, civil rights and voting rights group founded in Selma, Alabama, in the late 1920s.

Dallas County sheriff James G. Clark, Jr. epitomized white resistance to racial change in Selma in much the same way that Bull Connor did in Birmingham. Clark relished his role as a defender of segregation and made no attempt whatsoever to hide his preference for brutal policing methods. Clark's men wore 'old army fatigues, helmets, and boots, and the whole posse was empowered to carry weapons and make arrests', giving them a militia-like status.

White businessmen in Selma had taken some steps to address the situation. Fearing an SCLC campaign in Selma, they had held talks with local black leaders resulting in the removal of segregation signs from water fountains at the downtown courthouse. Selma had recently elected a new, young mayor,

Joseph Smitherman, who appeared to support efforts to move toward greater racial moderation. Smitherman had appointed a director of public safety, Wilson Baker, to try to restrain Clark and his men and to handle any civil rights demonstrations.

King and the SCLC knew that for a campaign to succeed in Selma it would need the full backing of the local black community and of SNCC, which had already laid claim to the city as its territory. However, unlike in Albany, SNCC was more receptive to SCLC involvement in the local movement at Selma. As SNCC's campaign faltered, local civil rights leader Amelia Platts Boynton, whose husband S. William Boynton had revived the Dallas County Voters League in 1936, approached King and the SCLC for assistance.

SNCC begrudgingly acquiesced to the request for King and the SCLC's help. As SNCC communications director Julian Bond explains, 'We would sometimes ask King to go someplace, because we knew the attention he drew would be helpful to the local scene, even if it wasn't helpful to us.'

When King arrived in Selma on 2 January 1965, he spoke to several hundred people at Brown Chapel AME Church, calling the city 'a symbol of bitter-end resistance in the South'. King's presence helped to bolster a flagging local movement. Local black lawyer J. L. Chestnut recalls that King 'gave the movement in Selma more legitimacy and raised the confidence factor' among local people.

On Monday morning, 18 January, King and SNCC chair John Lewis led 400 blacks to the county courthouse in an attempt to register them to vote. Scrupulously obeying the letter of law, they walked in groups of no more than four or five to avoid breaking the city's parade ordinance. Sheriff Clark, at the behest of Mayor Smitherman and director of public safety Wilson Baker, acted with restraint, asking the black voter registration applicants to wait in a nearby alley so that they could be called in one at a time to face the voter registration tests. Several hours later, however, not one black voter had been registered.

By the next day Clark's patience had already run out. He told Smitherman and Baker that he had had enough and that he 'was gonna arrest every so-and-so that came up here that day'. When a line of blacks waiting to register to vote at the city courthouse refused to move into a side alley as Clark instructed, the New York Times reported, Clark grabbed Amelia Platts Boynton 'by the back of her collar and pushed her roughly for half a block into a patrol car'. Boynton later confessed that at the time she 'didn't know whether I should go limp or whether I should turn around and knock him [Clark] out'. Clark's men made over 60 arrests that day.

Director of public safety Wilson Baker lamented that 'they [the movement] could depend upon him [Clark] from now to do anything they wanted him to do [and] they played him like an expert playing a violin.' A further

150 demonstrators were arrested the following day. On Friday 22 January, 100 black teachers marched on the courthouse to demonstrate against the unfair voter registration system.

James Bevel and other SCLC staff members believed that the time was right to bring the demonstrations to a head by having King submit to arrest. On 1 February, King led several hundred volunteers to the courthouse. Wilson Baker, who was aware of the movement's plans, made sure that he was on hand to supervise King's arrest rather than leaving it to Clark. Baker's men halted the march before its arrival at the courthouse and made 260 arrests.

Later that day, Clark arrested 700 demonstrators at the courthouse. In a first step to expand the movement to surrounding counties, SCLC organized a march by 600 blacks in Marion, Perry County, 50 miles from Selma. From a Selma jail cell, King kept in close contact with developments, handing detailed instructions to Andrew Young about what the movement should do next and insisting that demonstrations should not be called off until he had personally been consulted first.

On Thursday 4 February, Judge Thomas issued instructions to help facilitate the registration of black voters. These included dropping the existing voter registration tests, ignoring minor errors on application forms, and registering at least 100 black voters every day. Thomas also ordered Clark to desist from impeding prospective black voters from assembling at the courthouse.

Soon after Thomas's order, President Johnson issued a strong public statement in support of black voting rights. The interventions of Thomas and Johnson left King and the SCLC with a difficult choice to make. If they continued with demonstrations they would stand accused of not giving efforts to improve the situation in Selma a chance to work. However, past experience had shown that if they halted demonstrations they risked the local movement losing momentum and even coming to a standstill. Reluctantly, Andrew Young decided to suspend demonstrations.

When Young informed King, King told Young he had made the wrong decision. King instead insisted that the SCLC should step up rather than step back from demonstrations. 'Don't be too soft,' he told Young. 'We have the offensive. . . . In a crisis we must have a sense of drama. Don't let Baker control our movement.'

The following morning an advertisement appeared in the *New York Times* entitled 'A Letter from Martin Luther King from a Selma, Alabama, Jail'. Explicitly drawing a parallel between events in Selma and the earlier 1963 Birmingham Campaign, when King had written his 'Letter From Birmingham City Jail', King appealed for financial contributions to help the movement and pointed out that 'THIS IS SELMA, ALABAMA. THERE ARE MORE NEGROES IN JAIL WITH ME THAN ARE ON THE VOTING ROLLS.'

King left jail on 5 February, as planned, on the same day that the *New York Times* advertisement appeared. He announced to reporters that he would be going to Washington DC to ask President Johnson for voting rights legislation. During their ten-minute meeting, Johnson assured King that he was already preparing to act in the area of black voting rights.

Johnson's assurance coupled with signs that demonstrations were beginning to take their toll convinced King to wind up the Selma Campaign while the movement was winning. King had been hospitalized in Atlanta suffering from exhaustion. The incarcerated James Bevel came down with a fever and was treated at a local Selma infirmary while still chained to his prison bed. Even Sheriff Clark was feeling the strain. He too was hospitalized, with chest pains. 'The niggers are giving me a heart attack,' he told friends.

Local movement leaders decided to target nearby Lowndes, Perry and Wilcox counties as the focus of new voter registration efforts to take the focus away from Selma. On Thursday 18 February, as part of the movement's new wave of demonstrations, SCLC's C. T. Vivian led local blacks in Marion, Perry County, down to the local courthouse. Local police, assisted by state troopers, attacked the demonstrators. One young black participant, Jimmie Lee Jackson, was shot and wounded by a state trooper while attempting to shield and protect his mother from attack. On 26 February, Jackson died in his hospital bed, the first person ever to be killed in demonstrations directly linked to an SCLC campaign.

Jackson's death reversed the movement's plans for a cooling-off period in Selma. Instead, King announced plans to dramatize the situation over the denial of black voting rights in Alabama, and to protest at Jackson's death, by organizing a mass motorcade from Selma to Alabama's seat of government at Montgomery. Later the plan was revised to a Selma-to-Montgomery march starting on Sunday 7 March.

Taking a group of blacks on foot through 54 miles of some of the most racist territory in the South was a hazardous, not to mention a physically arduous, undertaking. It was the symbolic intent of the march rather than its speedy completion, however, that was the most important concern of the movement. In reality, King and the SCLC believed they would not be allowed to proceed since Governor George Wallace had instructed state troop commanders to turn back the march before it left Selma.

King and the SCLC considered their response to Wallace's action. One option was to seek a court order that expressly permitted the march and compelled the state authorities to let them proceed. Another was to go ahead with the march, wait for a stand-off with state troopers to develop, and then either stand their ground or poignantly pause before turning back.

King and SCLC staff members pondered the question of whether or not King should personally lead the march. Threats against King's life were being taken seriously enough to elicit warnings from the FBI and Attorney General Nicholas Katzenbach. There were also more practical matters to take into account. The likely prospect of the march being halted and of the participants being arrested would put King out of commission when his influence as a national lobbyist for voting rights legislation might be most needed. King considered delaying the march because of this, but both SCLC's James Bevel and Hosea Williams stressed that a delay would weaken its impact. King therefore tentatively agreed that the march should go ahead in his absence.

On the day of the march, with 600 movement supporters already gathered at Brown Chapel, SCLC staff remained uncertain of their exact plans. As expected, state troopers had been deployed across the city's Edmund Pettus Bridge to block the march route to Montgomery. Some SCLC staff suggested that they should take a different route to avoid the state troopers. Others insisted that they should not back down from a confrontation. From Atlanta, King advised that the march should proceed along the planned route.

SCLC staff drew lots to see who would lead. Hosea Williams won the dubious honour. SNCC chair John Lewis took his place alongside Williams at the front of the march. At Edmund Pettus Bridge, as the marchers reached the crest they could see the state troopers lined up on the other side waiting for them.

When the marchers reached the state troopers, troop commander Major John Cloud halted them. 'This is an unlawful assembly,' Cloud told the marchers. 'You are ordered to disperse and go back to your church or to your home.' Three times Hosea Williams asked to speak with the major. Three times Cloud replied that 'There is no word to be had.' Cloud then told the marchers, 'You have two minutes to turn around and go back to your church.' One minute later, Cloud shouted, 'Troopers, advance.'

The state troopers charged the marchers. John Lewis, at the front of the march, later remembered, 'The troopers came toward us with billyclubs, tear gas, and bullwhips, trampling us with horses.' Eight-year-old Sheyann Webb, King's 'smallest freedom fighter' in Selma, recalled, 'I saw these horsemen coming toward me and they had those awful [gas] masks on; they rode right through the cloud of tear gas . . . Some of them had clubs, others had ropes or whips, which they swung about them like they were driving cattle. . . . People were running and falling and ducking and you could hear the horses' hooves on the pavement and you'd hear people scream and hear the whips swishing and you'd hear them striking the people. They'd cry out; some moaned.' As Webb was retreating, Hosea Williams picked her up and put her under his arm to carry her to safety.

Cloud's men forced the marchers back to Brown Chapel in the heart of the black community. The white invasion of the black neighbourhood brought black residents out into the streets with 'shotguns and rifles and pistols'. By the time the conflict ended there were over 70 hospitalizations including 'fractured ribs and wrists, severe head gashes, broken teeth', and the suspected fractured skull of John Lewis.

Television footage of events made sensational viewing for the nation that evening. The American Broadcasting Company (ABC) interrupted its feature film *Judgement at Nuremberg* about Nazi war crime trials to show coverage of events at Selma. Andrew Young noted that '[M]any viewers apparently mistook those clips for portions of the Nuremberg film.' The photographs of events in Selma that appeared on the front pages of national newspapers the following morning reinforced the national outrage at events.

King was stung by the subsequent criticism about his absence. He had expected that the police would use mass arrests rather than mass violence to break up the march. King appealed to movement supporters nationwide to bombard the President and Congress with telegrams to protest against events in Selma and for them to converge on the city for a second attempt to march from Selma to Montgomery the following Tuesday. This time, King would be there at the front to lead.

SCLC attorneys went to Federal District Judge Frank Johnson to ask him to bar interference with Tuesday's march and in Congress there was widespread condemnation of events in Selma. Attorney General Nicholas Katzenbach later told Selma's director of public safety Wilson Baker that 'You people [in Selma] passed [the 1965 Voting Rights Act] on that bridge that Sunday.'

When King arrived in Selma on the Monday evening before the march, he was greeted with the news that Judge Johnson wanted it delayed so that he could hold hearings about issuing a restraining order against interference with it. Judge Johnson told movement officials that if they went ahead with the march irrespective of his wishes, he would issue an order to expressly forbid it from taking place.

King was inclined to postpone the march to stay on the right side of the law, but when he later addressed a mass rally at Brown Chapel, he reluctantly declared that the march would go ahead. King feared that if he cancelled the march the anger at events simmering in the local black community might spill over into violence. Going ahead offered a constructive and, importantly, a non-violent way for local people to vent their anger. 'It was one of the most painful decisions I ever made,' King later recalled. '[T]o try on the one hand to do what I felt was a practical matter of controlling a potentially explosive situation, and at the same time, not to defy a federal court order.'

Movement attorneys and Assistant Attorney General John Doar, President Johnson's representative in Selma, were confused by King's apparent change of heart. They believed that they already had a tacit agreement with King to delay Tuesday's march in return for an eventual restraining order against inter-ference with it. President Johnson dispatched **Community Relations Service**

Community Relations Service: Part of the Department of Justice formed by the 1964 Civil Rights Act to mediate community conflict.

(CRS) director LeRoy Collins and his staff member A. M. Secrest to Selma to negotiate a solution.

On Tuesday morning, Collins, Secrest, two fellow CRS workers already on the scene and John Doar, went to visit an unrepentant King. Desperate to avoid a repeat of the scenes witnessed the previous Sunday, the federal representatives suggested a compromise. Under the compromise agreement, the march would begin as planned. However, when the marchers reached state troopers on Edmund Pettus Bridge, the marchers would turn around and go back to Brown Chapel to wait for the court's restraining order to be handed down. When that court order had been handed down the march would then be able to proceed lawfully and unhindered.

The federal representatives hoped that this would satisfy movement demands for the march to go ahead while at the same time placating Judge Johnson. King was agreeable but expressed doubts over whether SNCC or state troopers could be persuaded to back down if the seemingly inevitable confrontation between them arose. King agreed to talk over the plan with SNCC and local movement leaders and Collins agreed to work on the state troopers to uphold their end of the bargain not to attack demonstrators.

Later, as King waited at Brown Chapel to begin the march, news came through that Judge Johnson had issued an order banning it. King had never broken a federal court order before. But he decided to proceed with the march. Many people from across the country, black and white, had responded to the SCLC's call for help and had arrived in Selma to join the march. To tell them the march was cancelled, King reasoned, would be a serious blow to the movement's prestige nationally as well as locally. Added to this, SNCC had already decided that the march was going to go ahead with or without King. If King participated he could at least exert some degree of control over events.

Around 2,000 marchers set off. As they reached Edmund Pettus Bridge a US marshal stopped King and read out Judge Johnson's order banning the march. King and the marchers ignored the order and proceeded on over the bridge to face Alabama state troopers. When King and the marchers reached the state troopers, King stopped, knelt down and held prayers. After singing the movement anthem 'We Shall Overcome', King turned around to lead the marchers back to Brown Chapel.

At that very moment, the state troopers blocking the road ahead to Montgomery moved aside inviting the marchers to proceed. It was a calculated act designed to embarrass King. Nevertheless, King stuck to his word and led the marchers back to Brown Chapel.

Back at Brown Chapel, King had to tread a delicate line. He did not want to admit that a deal had been done with Collins to turn around since he feared the inevitable SNCC charge that he had sold the local movement short. At the same time, King did not want to deny the deal, since it offered a potential future defence against a contempt of court citation from Judge Johnson. Later, King explained away what SNCC dubbed the 'Tuesday Turnaround' by insisting that it had been instigated 'because we felt we had made our point, we had revealed the continued presence of violence'.

That evening, as supporters of the movement continued to flood into Selma, local whites at the Silver Moon Café attacked white Boston minister Rev. James B. Reeb who was walking back from downtown with two other ministers. Two days later, Reeb died from his injuries, becoming the second fatality of the Selma Campaign. Nationwide, marches in many of the United States' major cities demonstrated widespread support for the local movement in Selma. Congressmen lined up to condemn events in Alabama and President Johnson hurried efforts to frame voting rights legislation. When Judge Johnson's hearing on events began on Thursday, King finally admitted that he had brokered a deal with Collins to turn the march around.

On Monday, President Johnson gave a special televised address to Congress in which he unequivocally threw his support behind black voting rights and behind the civil rights movement. Significantly, Johnson used the movement's own words to insist to the nation that 'We Shall Overcome'. King, in Selma for Rev. James Reeb's memorial service, watched the speech on television. It brought tears to his eyes. The NAACP's Roy Wilkins was similarly moved, recalling that 'I had waited all my life to hear a President of the United States talk that way.'

White southerners saw Johnson's speech very differently. 'I almost went limp, I was weak,' remembers Selma's mayor Smitherman, on hearing Johnson's speech. 'When he said "We Shall Overcome" it was just as though somebody had just stuck a knife in your heart.' Smitherman felt that 'it's over with now . . . our President's sold us out.'

On Wednesday 17 March, President Johnson introduced his Voting Rights bill to Congress. Its central proposal was to provide the US attorney general with the power to cancel all literacy and voting rights tests and to appoint federal registrars to actively assist black voters. This applied to all areas where less than 50 per cent of the population had been registered voters, or where less than 50 per cent of the population had actually cast ballots, in the previous presidential election. The formula covered Alabama, Georgia, Louisiana, Mississippi, North and South Carolina, and Virginia, although it left out Arkansas, Florida, Tennessee and Texas.

The bill met with swift action in the US Senate but in an indication of the delaying power of the southern states in the US House of Representatives – not inconsequentially, a power that was itself a product of the corrupt voting rights practices that the bill sought to put an end to – the bill did not become law until August 1965 [**Doc. 16, p. 149**].

On the same day that the voting rights bill was introduced to Congress, in Montgomery Judge Frank Johnson concluded his hearings about the disturbances in Selma and agreed to let the march proceed. King and the SCLC announced that the new march would begin on Sunday 21 March. Since the voting rights bill had already been introduced to Congress, the courts had already affirmed the right of the march to proceed, and the federal government had already arranged protection for the marchers, the march from Selma to Montgomery became a victory parade rather than a demonstration.

King led the march, which culminated at Montgomery on Thursday 25 March. The occasion marked a homecoming of sorts, bringing King back to the site of the Montgomery bus boycott, which he had led as president of the MIA nine years earlier. Yet despite the celebration, the day witnessed the third fatality of the Selma Campaign. White Detroit housewife Viola Gregg Liuzzo was shot and killed by Ku Klux Klan members in Lowndes County as she ferried movement workers back to Selma from Montgomery. As so often in the civil rights movement, temporary victories were quickly followed by the harsh realities of ongoing hostility to change.

Further reading

The best overview of the Selma Campaign and its relation to the 1965 Voting Rights Act is David J. Garrow, *Protest at Selma: Martin Luther King, Jr., and the Voting Rights Act of 1965* (1978). Several first-hand accounts include black lawyer J. L. Chestnut, Jr., with Julia Cass, *Black in Selma: The Uncommon Life of J. L. Chestnut, Jr.* (1991), white minister Richard D. Leonard, *Call to Selma: Eighteen Days of Witness*, and two black schoolgirls involved in the campaign, Sheyann Webb and Rachel West Nelson, *Selma, Lord, Selma: Girlhood Memories of the Civil Rights Days* (1980). Two studies examine the death of white housewife Viola Liuzzo in the aftermath of the Selma to Montgomery march: Gary May, *The Informant: The FBI, the Ku Klux Klan, and the Murder of Viola Liuzzo* (2005) and Mary Stanton, *From Selma to Sorrow: The Life and Death of Viola Liuzzo* (1998). On rural civil rights struggles see Cynthia Griggs Fleming, *In the Shadow of Selma: The Continuing Struggle for Civil Rights in the Rural South* (2004). On the impact of the voting rights act see Chandler Davidson and Bernard Grofman, eds., *Quite Revolution in the South: The Impact of the Voting Right Act, 1965–1990* (1994); Gordon A. Martin, Jr., *Count Them One by One: Black Mississippians Fighting for the Right to Vote* (2010); and Frank Parker, *Black Votes Count: Political Empowerment in Mississippi after 1965* (1990).

Part 5

KING AND A FRACTIOUS
MOVEMENT, 1965–1968

11

The Chicago Campaign, 1965–1966

With Selma and the Voting Rights Act one phase of development in the civil rights revolution came to an end,' reflected King in 1967. 'A new phase opened, but few observers realized it or were prepared for its implications.' In truth, King only understood this with the benefit of hindsight. 'When the 1965 SCLC convention took place in August in Birmingham,' admits SCLC's Andrew Young, 'we really didn't know what our direction should be after Selma.' A. Philip Randolph termed the movement's condition a 'crisis of victory'.

When the Voting Rights Act passed in August 1965, the movement had succeeded in gaining federal legislation in response to two of its central demands: the desegregation of public facilities and accommodations and the enforcement of black voting rights. The Selma Campaign had witnessed an unprecedented degree of public support, indicated both in opinion polls and in the numbers of whites actually willing to participate in civil rights marches and demonstrations. The federal government had provided the movement in Selma with more assistance than at any time in the past. The challenge now was to devise a programme that could tap latent support for civil rights and take the movement on to its next stage of development – whatever that might be.

As was often the case in the movement, events outside of their control shaped King and the SCLC's next major campaign. On 11 August 1965, just five days after President Johnson signed the Voting Rights Act into law, a riot broke out in Watts, a predominantly black district of Los Angeles, after an altercation between local black residents and a white state highway patrolman. The riot, which lasted for six days and resulted in 35 deaths, was the most serious outbreak of race-related violence in the United States since the civil rights movement had begun. Racial disturbances in New York, Philadelphia and Rochester the previous year were forewarnings of the potentially explosive mounting black frustration and anger in America's cities.

After some hesitation about becoming involved, King finally accepted the invitation of black clergymen in Los Angeles to visit the city. King was appalled by the devastation caused by the riots and by the desperation of the local black population living in squalid urban conditions. Yet he found few blacks in Watts willing to listen to his message of non-violence. Instead, local residents put forward their own 'Watts Manifesto' of 'Burn, Baby Burn'. King later reflected that 'The situation in Watts erupted in volcanic form, because the people there knew or felt that their deep troubles were interlaced with manifest injustice. And this eruption potential is just below the surface in portions of almost every large city in the U.S.'

King came away from Watts convinced that the SCLC must now turn its full attention to the plight of urban blacks in America's major cities that had been largely overlooked in a hitherto southern-based small town and small city movement. Over the summer of 1965, King set out on a People-to-People tour of northern cities including Cleveland, New York, Philadelphia, Washington DC and Chicago.

Out of these places, Chicago emerged as the most promising target for King and the SCLC's first northern campaign. The city appealed for a number of reasons. King called it 'the Birmingham of the North', believing that it symbolized black northern problems in 1965 in the same way that Birmingham had symbolized black southern problems in 1963. King also believed that if the SCLC could tackle the problems blacks faced in Chicago it could provide a blueprint for tackling similar problems faced by blacks in other northern cities, just as the Birmingham Campaign had provided a blueprint for black protest in the South.

Since the early decades of the twentieth century, Chicago had been one of a number of northern cities that acted as magnets for southern black migrants in search of perceived better opportunities. By 1960, it was the second biggest city in the US and over 1 million of its 3.5 million inhabitants were black. However, blacks in Chicago found themselves mired in a pervasive system of racial discrimination. The development of black ghettos to the south and the west of the city was a cauldron for a whole host of interconnected problems: poor housing, high unemployment, crime, drugs and youth gangs.

Despite the existence of these problems, rents and house prices in the ghettos were extortionately high. Unscrupulous white landlords and city real estate brokers colluded to keep them that way. Blacks who attempted to move into white neighbourhoods met with violent resistance. What effectively constituted segregated housing in Chicago, enforced in practice if not by law, led to *de facto* segregated schools and other facilities that were located in black neighbourhoods.

De Facto Segregation: Segregation that is enforced by or emerges from both formal and informal practices that are not explicitly sanctioned by law.

King and the SCLC were optimistic about running a campaign in the city for a number of reasons. Chicago mayor Richard J. Daley fronted an influential local Democratic Party that dominated the city's affairs. Daley had been supportive of the civil rights movement in the past and had spoken at a civil rights rally in the city in 1963 after the SCLC's Birmingham Campaign. King believed that if he could persuade the mayor of the need to do more to tackle the problems that his black constituents faced, Daley might act to implement reform.

Chicago's strong white unions and the prominent role of the Catholic Church in the city formed two other potential constituencies of sympathetic white liberal support. In the black community, the existence of a strong local civil rights organization, the **Coordinating Council of Community Organizations (CCCO)**, which actively welcomed SCLC's presence, also appeared to be in King and the SCLC's favour. King and the SCLC joined the CCCO, headed by Albert Raby, in an alliance under the banner of the **Chicago Freedom Movement (CFM)**.

Coordinating Council of Community Organizations: Local Chicago civil rights organization founded in 1962.

Chicago Freedom Movement: A coalition of organizations that joined together to run the 1965–1966 Chicago Campaign.

The fact that two of the SCLC's most dynamic figures, one old, one new, were based in Chicago, gave the city added appeal. James Bevel had taken a leave of absence from SCLC in 1965 to become programme director of the West Side Christian Parish, an inner-city outreach ministry in the West Side of Chicago. Jesse Jackson, a relative newcomer to SCLC, but one of its fast-rising stars, was SCLC's main contact in the South Side of Chicago. Jackson became involved with the civil rights movement during 1963 demonstrations in Greensboro, North Carolina. A year later he moved north to study at the Chicago Theological Seminary. In 1965, Jackson took part in the Selma Campaign, and when the SCLC began to turn its attention to Chicago, he became involved in its activities there.

Given the scale and depth of the problems of racial discrimination in Chicago, King and the SCLC proposed a different sort of approach to that city from that in previous campaigns. Before engaging in non-violent direct action demonstrations, King and the SCLC planned a period of fact-finding, community organizing, and community education, to allow the organization to get to grips with the problems blacks faced in the city and to try to come up with ways in which they might be addressed. James Bevel liaised with local blacks in the West Side of Chicago and developed a programme for a 'Union to End Slums' by organizing ghetto tenants on a block-by-block basis.

Jesse Jackson liaised with local blacks in the South Side of Chicago and developed two different programmes. Firstly, he helped to found and then led the Kenwood-Oakland Community Organization in one South Side neighbourhood. Secondly, he helped to enlist the support of Chicago's black ministers. Wary of Bevel's more radical tenant organizing campaign, black ministers were persuaded, under Jackson's direction, to launch '**Operation Breadbasket**', which used selective buying campaigns as a leverage to elicit better black job opportunities from employers.

Operation Breadbasket: SCLC initiative from 1962 to 1972 that was dedicated to improving the economic conditions in black communities.

Owing to the different SCLC approach in Chicago, King's own involvement in its early stages was slight. Andrew Young announced the start of the

SCLC's Chicago campaign on 1 September 1965, but it was not until 5 January 1966 that King made his first appearance in the city. Even then, King did not commit to Chicago on a full-time basis, although he did vow to try to spend at least three days a week there. King moved into a rundown apartment on the third floor of a building at 1550 South Hamlin Avenue in Chicago's West Side in an attempt to graphically illustrate existing slum conditions.

When the management discovered that King was moving in, it quickly got to work redecorating and repairing the place to try to make it more habitable. This prompted one Chicago newspaper to facetiously suggest that if King simply adopted the tactic of moving from apartment to apartment all of the slums would eventually disappear. Yet when King, Coretta and their children moved into their new temporary home on 26 January, conditions in the apartment were still extremely poor. '[I]t was grim,' Coretta simply recalls.

King's first attempt to focus attention on or dramatize the problems of Chicago's slums came when he seized an apartment building at 1321 South Homan, in what he termed a 'supralegal trusteeship' of the building. Arrangements were made for the tenants to withhold rent money and instead to pool funds for repairs to the building. Questioned about the legality of the move, King replied that 'The moral question is far more important than the legal one.'

The ploy soon backfired. The Chicago press condemned the seizure of property and Chicago's Cook County Welfare Department withheld its rent subsidy to the tenants. Things were made even worse when it turned out that the owner of the building was John Bender, a white, poor, sick 81-year-old, who was hardly the epitome of the slum landlord that King had hoped he would be. 'I think King is right,' Bender told reporters. 'I think his intentions are right and in his place I'd do the same thing.'

The city charged Bender with 23 housing code violations. Three months later the courts ordered the building to be returned to its owner. Bender died shortly afterwards. During their period of occupation, SCLC spent $2,000 on repairs and collected only $200 in rent. The whole episode was a public relations disaster.

Almost eight months after Andrew Young had announced the beginning of SCLC's Chicago Campaign, the organization had precious little to show for its efforts. It was not that the campaign was an abject failure: Bevel and Jackson were making steady progress in their respective projects and other SCLC staff members were hard at work. It was more that the SCLC's approach to the Chicago Campaign highlighted exactly why King and the SCLC had made the type of contribution to the civil rights movement that they had in the past: short-term black community mobilizing in a non-violent direct action campaign was what they were most suited to and what they did best.

In certain respects, King and the SCLC were also hostages to their own fortunes. The drama and spectacle of each past campaign set a benchmark and raised expectations for the next. The newsworthiness of King and his national prestige were in many ways the SCLC's main asset. The day-to-day trudge of community organizing lacked the glamour and excitement that could attract the media and focus attention on King. It was felt that there was a need to return to the type of campaign that King and the SCLC had run in the past, which played to their strengths. The issues needed simplification and focus in order to dramatize them and to put King at the forefront. Plans were made to launch a non-violent direct action campaign that would concentrate attention on the inability of blacks to escape the ghetto by bringing that problem quite literally to the doorsteps of whites in a number of 'open housing' marches through white neighbourhoods.

On 10 July King led a rally at Chicago's Soldier Field and afterwards marched downtown to tape the movement demands on the door of City Hall, a move evoking the actions of his namesake, church reformer Martin Luther, who nailed his 95 Theses to the door of Castle Church in Wittenberg in 1517 [Doc. 17, p. 150].

The next day, King and local movement representatives met with Mayor Daley. Daley insisted that the city was doing its best to tackle the problems of the slums, and movement representatives insisted that they were ready to engage in non-violent direct action to compel the city to do more. That night, the SCLC announced that the non-violent direct action phase of the Chicago Campaign would begin by targeting housing discrimination in Gage Park, one of Chicago's exclusively white neighbourhoods.

Events on the ground in Chicago soon overtook the movement's plans. In the middle of a sweltering Midwest heatwave children in black neighbourhoods had turned on fire hydrants for spray to cool down, a not uncommon practice in the city. On 12 July, Chicago fire commissioner Robert Quinn ordered the fire hydrants to be turned off to stop the city's water pressure from falling. Attempts to enforce this policy led to conflict between police and local black residents that rapidly escalated into a full pitched battle.

King first learned of what was happening when he and Coretta witnessed gangs of black youths running in the streets. He immediately went down to the local police station to try to secure the release of six arrested black youths. Successful in this endeavour, he then headed to the black Shiloh Baptist Church to show local residents that he had secured their release and to insist that they should put an end to the violence. Few were willing to listen. They angrily denounced the Chicago police for its actions and refused to listen to King's appeal for calm. Instead, they drifted outside to join a growing and hostile crowd of blacks. King was powerless to contain their anger.

Over the next few days a full-scale riot developed. Violence erupted in the very areas of the West Side ghetto where the SCLC had worked for almost a year. On 15 July, with two people dead, Illinois governor Otto Kerner called out the National Guard. King attempted to stop the violence by getting local movement leaders and ministers to talk with the rioters, but this too met with little success. 'A lot of people have lost faith in the establishment,' King conceded. 'They have lost faith in the democratic process.'

Negotiations between the movement and Mayor Daley produced only token measures to address the short-term problems of the black community. Daley ordered fire hydrants to be turned back on and for mobile swimming pools to be shipped into black neighbourhoods. Chicago news columnist Mike Royko sardonically noted Daley's determination to make 'Chicago's blacks the wettest in the country'. One local black activist mused, 'I think they're hoping we'll all grow gills and swim away.'

To King and local movement leaders the rioting demonstrated the need to direct the anger and frustration felt by Chicago blacks into more peaceful and constructive channels. Over the following weeks, leading SCLC figures and local movement leaders launched non-violent direct action demonstrations. They picketed selected Chicago real estate firms and held 'Open Housing' marches into white neighbourhoods. The violence they encountered, with whites throwing rocks and bottles at them and wrecking their parked vehicles, evoked images of the SCLC's southern campaigns and effectively demonstrated that white prejudice and bigotry were just as present in the North as in the South.

As the campaign gathered momentum, King led his first open housing march, targeting four real estate firms in the Gage Park and Chicago Lawn neighbourhoods. A caravan of 600 people in over 100 cars travelled to join him. Over 1,000 police officers were dispatched to offer the marchers protection.

However, despite the considerable police presence, shortly after emerging from his car King was struck by a rock on the side of the head. After taking a few moments to recover, he continued the march through a volley of missiles. By the end of the march, police had made 41 arrests and 30 marchers had been injured. King told the press that he had 'been in many demonstrations all across the South, but I can say that I have never – even in Mississippi and Alabama – seen mobs as hostile and hate-filled as I've seen in Chicago.'

Amid ongoing demonstrations Mayor Daley agreed to attend two 'Summit Conferences' on Wednesday 17 August and Friday 26 August with movement leaders and leading white community figures, organized by the interracial Chicago Conference on Religion and Race. Daley and city real estate representatives made a number of non-discriminatory pledges at the summit meetings but offered little by way of concrete concessions. However, with violence escalating and the courts making moves to ban further open housing marches, King felt it was time to take what was on the table, announce victory and leave.

An upbeat King told the press afterwards that the Summit Agreement would mean 'the total eradication of housing discrimination' in Chicago and that all further marches would be halted. Not everyone in the movement was so confident. James Bevel told the press that he would have to 'think about' whether he was happy with the agreement or not. Others were less reserved. Local black leader Chester Robinson declared that 'We feel the poor Negro has been sold out by this agreement.'

There were many in Chicago who agreed with Robinson's sentiments. Subsequent events bore out the fears of local leaders that the city had no intention of carrying out the terms of its agreement. Over the ensuing months there was little apparent change in the city's housing practices. Attempts by the SCLC to sponsor a voter registration campaign to pressure the city to live up to its commitments failed miserably. Hosea Williams, placed in charge of the campaign, claimed 32,000 new black registrations. The city put the figure nearer to 320.

A distinct lack of federal pressure for change undermined King and the SCLC's efforts even further. In September 1966, attempts to pass the 1966 civil rights bill, which included provisions for fair housing, had finally failed. In April 1967, Mayor Daley was returned to office, winning over four-fifths of the black vote. With Daley's political career intact he ignored all of the city's previous commitments. The local movement fell apart.

The Chicago Campaign contained some prescient indicators for King, the SCLC and the civil rights movement. The complex and multifaceted problems of structural racism that King found in Chicago were not susceptible to the tactics that King and the SCLC had used in the southern-based campaigns. Northern liberal supporters of the civil rights movement in the South, like Mayor Daley, were much less sympathetic to demonstrations in their own cities in the North. The same was true of groups like the unions and the Catholic Church in Chicago, which although potential allies in the South were more likely to side with their own white working-class constituencies in the North.

Moreover, King and the SCLC discovered, the black community in the North was different from that in the South. Black leaders there were already absorbed into city politics rather than excluded altogether, and therefore more inclined to work within the system than to protest against it. King's authority as a Baptist preacher was less certain among younger urban blacks. The sheer physical scale of Chicago proved overwhelming: the city was ten times bigger than Birmingham and 100 times bigger than Selma.

When King and the SCLC left Chicago they were still largely where they had been at the beginning of the campaign, knowing that the movement had entered a new phase of development, but not knowing how to modify their past tactics to meet present demands. Elsewhere, others in the movement were developing their own tactics and responses to the new challenges ahead.

Further reading

Two books provide overviews of the Chicago Campaign: Alan B. Anderson and George W. Pickering, *Confronting the Color Line: The Broken Promise of the Civil Rights Movement in Chicago* (1986) and James R. Ralph, Jr., *Northern Protest: Martin Luther King, Jr., Chicago, and the Civil Rights Movement* (1993). Far more attention has shifted to the national rather than the exclusively southern dimensions of the civil rights movement in recent years. A useful starting point to explore this phenomenon is Thomas Sugrue, *Sweet Land of Liberty: The Forgotten Struggle for Civil Rights in the North* (2008). On housing segregation see Stephen Grant Meyer, *As Long As They Don't Move Next Door: Segregation and Racial Conflict in American Neighborhoods* (2000). On the white conservative backlash to the civil rights movement and its long-term consequences see Dan T. Carter, *The Politics of Rage: George Wallace, the Origins of the New Conservatism, and the Transformation of American Politics* (1995).

12

The Meredith March Against Fear and Black Power, 1966

On 5 June 1966, James Meredith set out from Memphis, Tennessee, on a '**March Against Fear**' through Mississippi to the state capital of Jackson. Meredith had desegregated the University of Mississippi in 1962 amid a great deal of controversy. White resistance to Meredith's admission to the university had resulted in clashes between a white mob and federal marshals and a federalized Mississippi National Guard. The white mob had wounded 160 federal marshals and killed two people.

Meredith's plan to march across Mississippi was essentially a personal protest befitting his reputation as something of a civil rights maverick. The march would inevitably expose Meredith to personal danger. He was one of the most well-known black activists in Mississippi and planned to walk alone through some of the most hostile rural territory in the South. On the second day of his march, Meredith was felled by two shotgun blasts. The resulting injuries were not serious, but they did mean that the march looked like coming to a premature end while Meredith recovered from his wounds in a Memphis hospital.

King was in an SCLC meeting when he heard the news about the Meredith shooting. There was 'a momentary hush of anger and dismay throughout the room', King recalled, as early reports suggested that Meredith had been killed. As relief at the news that Meredith had only been wounded arrived, King and other civil rights leaders resolved to continue the march Meredith had begun.

On 7 June, King, new CORE national director Floyd McKissick, and newly elected SNCC chair Stokely Carmichael, met with Meredith in his hospital room. King, McKissick and Carmichael 'spent some time discussing the character and logistics of the march and agreed that we would consult him [Meredith] on every decision'.

Meredith gave his blessing for the march to continue. That afternoon, 21 people drove to the spot where Meredith had been shot and resumed the

March Against Fear: Instigated by James Meredith in 1966 as an individual protest to assert his right to free movement in the state, after his shooting it was continued with the support of all of the major civil rights organizations.

march. They had walked barely 50 yards before Mississippi highway patrolmen forced them off the road, telling participants that they did not have a permit to march and that they would therefore have to walk at the side of the road.

After some pushing and shoving as patrolmen physically removed the marchers from the road, King calmed tempers by insisting that it would be better for the march to continue peacefully than not to continue at all. Later, spirits began to lift as the marchers covered six miles to the small town of Coldwater, Mississippi, without impediment.

That night, the marchers returned to Memphis, holding a rally at James Lawson's Centenary Methodist Church. The NAACP's Roy Wilkins and the National Urban League's Whitney Young joined them afterwards to discuss strategy and tactics for the march. They were ready to back the protest as a means of focusing national attention on efforts to pass the 1966 civil rights bill in Congress.

New SNCC chair Carmichael objected to their presence. He rang out a list of demands that were unacceptable to them. The march should focus on its original intention of eliminating black fear and not on national legislation, Carmichael said. If there was to be any mention of legislation, it should highlight the shortcomings of Johnson's existing proposals and not support them.

Moreover, Carmichael insisted that groups advocating armed self-defence, such as Louisiana's **Deacons for Defense and Justice**, should be welcome on the march. Carmichael even castigated Wilkins and Young directly, using colourful and abrasive language and making it clear that he believed that the older and more conservative civil rights leaders were out of touch with the current direction of the movement. Irate at Carmichael's onslaught and King's apparent unwillingness to leap to their defence, Wilkins and Young left the meeting and returned to New York.

Deacons for Defense and Justice: Louisiana civil rights organization that advocated armed self-defence.

The departure of Wilkins and Young was part of a carefully contrived strategy by Carmichael. His rise in the SNCC reflected a significant shift in the organization away from its initial emphasis on non-violence and inter-racialism, and towards an embrace of black nationalism, black separatism and black armed self-defence. Carmichael had previously helped to found the Lowndes County Freedom Organization in Alabama as an independent expression of black political strength.

Disillusioned with coalition politics, Carmichael called for a focus on raising black consciousness and the promotion of race solidarity and race pride. Only when the black community built its own political, economic and cultural institutions, Carmichael believed, could it truly begin to address its position of powerlessness in American society.

This new direction marginalized the role whites played in SNCC. By the end of 1966, SNCC had effectively expelled all whites from the organization. Hand in hand with this shift in its civil rights objectives was a shift in tactics.

Non-violence began to give way to an advocacy of armed self-defence. To SNCC workers in rural Alabama and Mississippi, the idea of non-violence seemed increasingly irrelevant in the face of extreme white violence. Though still prepared to entertain non-violence purely as a tactic, there was no longer the same ideological and moral commitment to it that King and the SCLC held. Carmichael's defeat of John Lewis for the SNCC chair in May 1966 both reflected, and acted as a further catalyst for, the shifting orientation of the organization [**Doc. 18, p. 150**].

To Carmichael, the Meredith March offered an ideal opportunity to publicize and rally support for the new SNCC regime. Getting rid of Wilkins and Young removed the influence of those conservative civil rights leaders. Exactly why King allowed this to happen is unclear. It has been suggested by some that he let his existing personal differences with Wilkins cloud his judgement on the matter. Others have suggested that King believed he could control SNCC better by appearing to side with its militancy over more conservative leaders. Whatever his motives, he did not seem to fully appreciate the extent to which Carmichael was manipulating the march for his own ends. Carmichael hoped to use King's kudos to publicize the march and to convince him to adopt a more radical stance.

When King and McKissick held a press conference on Wednesday 8 June, their march 'manifesto' bore the stamp of SNCC's uncompromising rhetoric. The document highlighted the failures and shortcomings of federal action rather than backing the new proposed legislation. The mood of the march when it began echoed those sentiments. 'I'm not for that nonviolence stuff anymore,' one student told King. 'If one of these damn white Mississippi crackers touches me, I'm gonna knock the hell out of him,' said another. Still others insisted that the movement's signature song should be changed from 'We Shall Overcome' to 'We Shall Overrun'.

Over the next few days the number of marchers grew to 400. As they came into contact with black communities they encouraged voter registration efforts and local civil rights activism. Despite their perceived differences with King, some SNCC workers were surprised at how well they got along with him. 'He turned out to be easygoing, with a delightful sense of humor,' noted Cleveland Sellers. 'His mind was open and we were surprised to find that he was much less conservative than we initially believed.'

Carmichael had known King for many years and remembered that 'When I went into Atlanta I would go and eat in his house. Our relationship was very strong even where we had political disagreements.' King left the march for Chicago on 10 June, returning briefly to Mississippi on Sunday 12 June, before leaving again to attend to SCLC business in Atlanta. He rejoined the march at Grenada, Mississippi, on 14 and 15 June, before leaving for Chicago again for the following two days.

King's frequent absences played into SNCC's hands by allowing it to set the tone for and to thereby seize control of the march. As King was away in Chicago on 16 June, the march headed to Greenwood, a long established centre of SNCC activism. That night, when Carmichael and others tried to pitch tents at a local black school, white public safety commissioner B. A. Hammond ordered them to leave. When they refused, they were arrested.

Later released on bail, an angry Carmichael went to Broad Street Park, where the city had finally allowed the marchers to set up camp. Carmichael told the marchers that 'every courthouse in Mississippi should be burnt down tomorrow so we can get rid of the dirt'. He insisted that black sheriffs should preside in predominantly black counties and that black citizens should hold political power. Then, putting a name to the new mood in SNCC, in a slogan already popularized on the march by SNCC worker Willie Ricks, Carmichael shouted, 'We want black power.' The crowd enthusiastically echoed his chant.

The following afternoon, King returned from Chicago to lead 1,000 marchers to the Leflore County Courthouse. After confronting Leflore County sheriff George Smith, march leaders successfully entered the building to hold a 20-minute meeting on voter registration.

At the evening rally in Greenwood, Willie Ricks once again took up the chant 'We want black power.' It was the first time King had heard the slogan, which he immediately found disconcerting. He felt that the phrase was 'an unfortunate choice of words' that was destined to widen existing divisions within the movement and to increase white hostility to it. Seeking to neutralize the chant, SCLC's Hosea Williams encouraged marchers to shout 'Freedom Now' instead.

Confirming King's fears, the rival chants quickly led to a contest to see which could be shouted the loudest. King was so concerned about the new development that he considered withdrawing SCLC from the march altogether. The controversy over Black Power among marchers meant that the event was beginning to highlight internal movement divisions more than it was dramatizing the need for civil rights.

King left the march for two more days, returning on Tuesday 21 June as marchers took a detour into Philadelphia, Mississippi, where SNCC workers James Chaney, Michael Schwerner and Andrew Goodman had been murdered two years earlier. As King led 250 marchers into town, in the absence of police protection local whites taunted and harassed them.

At the Neshoba County Courthouse, chief deputy sheriff Cecil Ray Price prevented marchers from holding a meeting on the courthouse lawn. King confronted him, asking, 'You're the one who had Schwerner and those fellows in jail?' Price proudly replied 'Yes, sir.' King's further attempts to hold a memorial service out in the street were heckled by 300 whites. Shaken, King declared that, 'I believe in my heart that the murderers are somewhere around me at this moment.' From behind him, Price muttered, 'You're damn right, they're right behind you right now.'

At a prearranged signal from Price's men, whites began to hurl bottles and firecrackers at the marchers. Fights broke out between local whites and some of the marchers, finally prompting local lawmen to intervene. Back at Mount Nebo Baptist Church, King told reporters that Philadelphia was 'the worst city I have ever seen. There is a complete reign of terror here.' He vowed to return with more marchers before the week was out.

The following day, march leaders talked tactics. They agreed that they should return to Philadelphia on Friday. Arrangements were also made for the conclusion of the march in Jackson on Sunday. What took up the most time, however, was a discussion about the use of the Black Power slogan. King pleaded with Carmichael and McKissick to drop the slogan, arguing that it would 'confuse our allies, isolate the Negro community and give many prejudiced whites, who might otherwise be ashamed of their anti-Negro feeling, a ready excuse for self-justification'.

They refused to listen to King, pointing to the slogan's popularity with local blacks in Mississippi. Ultimately, the two sides agreed to allow the slogan to remain while putting a stop to the shouting matches between the rival 'Black Power' and 'Freedom Now' chants. As the meeting broke up, Carmichael admitted to King, 'I deliberately decided to raise this issue on the march in order to give it a national forum and to force you to take a stand for Black Power.' King wearily replied, 'I have been used before. One more time won't hurt.'

On Thursday afternoon, the march wound up for the day in Canton where the Madison County sheriff arrested an advance party for trying to erect tents on the grounds of a local black school. When King and other march leaders arrived, they also attempted to make camp and to hold a rally on the school field.

A stand-off between the marchers and state highway patrolmen soon developed. The patrolmen tried to disperse the marchers by firing tear gas at them. King initially stood his ground but the gas finally overwhelmed him and other marchers who were forced to retreat. The state highway patrolmen removed the few remaining stragglers with the use of billyclubs.

The events infuriated march leaders since they had received federal assurances that state highway patrolmen would protect them on Friday's planned return to Philadelphia. Their sworn protectors for the following day now tear gassed them in Canton. Such duplicity undermined King's determined efforts to maintain a non-violent movement and instead only strengthened the appeal of armed self-defence.

'The government has got to give me some victories if I'm gonna keep people nonviolent,' King told white journalist Paul Good afterwards. 'I know

I'm gonna stay nonviolent no matter what happens. But a lot of people are getting hurt and bitter, and they can't see it that way anymore.' Even SCLC staff members were near the end of their tether. 'I didn't say it, but I thought to myself, "If I had a machine gun, I'd *show* those motherfuckers!"' recalls Andrew Young.

On Friday, the march through Philadelphia proved uneventful as state highway patrolmen successfully guarded demonstrators. It was back at Canton that afternoon, where marchers again threatened to pitch tents at the local black school, that there was most tension. Eventually, city officials compromised by telling march leaders that they could hold a rally at the school, but only if they agreed not to set up camp there. King left the decision to local black leaders, who agreed to the compromise. However, when the compromise was announced at the rally, many march participants booed the decision as a needless climbdown.

Saturday brought more dissensions. James Meredith, back for the final stages of the march, felt slighted when march leaders completed the penultimate leg from Canton to Tougaloo College on the outskirts of Jackson without him. Meredith angrily set out walking on his own from Canton. When SCLC's Andrew Young and Robert Green went to try to smooth relations, Meredith pushed them aside. Meredith's temper only calmed when King went to personally apologize and to accompany him on the final mile into Tougaloo.

That evening, there was more disagreement over who should be allowed to speak at Sunday's rally. National Urban League executive director Whitney Young was back and ready to endorse the march manifesto in return for a place on the podium. Though this was accepted, a similar courtesy to Mississippi NAACP state president Charles Evers was not. Evers, whose brother Medgar had been shot and killed in Jackson three years previously, had vacillated over his support for the march. Charles was now ready to lend his endorsement but the national NAACP still refused to sign up to the march manifesto. Above the protests of King and the SCLC, leaders from SNCC, CORE and the MFDP vetoed the appearance of an NAACP speaker without backing from the national organization.

On Sunday, the marchers took the eight-mile journey into Jackson. Somewhere between 12,000 and 16,000 people reportedly attended the rally, which turned out to be a prickly affair. Whites gathered to heckle the speakers and bitter wrangling over the 'Freedom Now' and 'Black Power' chants continued to divide movement activists.

The march ended in further acrimony when it appeared that the SCLC was being left to foot the bill for march expenses. Moreover, there was no consensus between the participating civil rights organizations about how to successfully follow up on the march. Consequently the SCLC, SNCC and NAACP made their own separate arrangements for voter registration drives in Mississippi. Unlike earlier civil rights demonstrations, where latent tensions between various civil rights organizations had often been papered over to give at least a semblance of unity, the infighting on the Meredith March was laid bare for all to see.

'The phrase "civil rights movement" lay moribund, dead forever with the birth of Black Power,' writes SNCC's James Forman in his autobiography. To be sure, Black Power seemed to successfully alienate core constituencies of civil rights movement support. Key federal supporters of the civil rights movement including President Johnson, Vice President Hubert Humphrey, and Senator Robert Kennedy, all condemned it. *Time* magazine labelled it the 'new racism' that was 'almost indistinguishable from the wild-eyed doctrines of the Black Muslims'.

Even black supporters of the civil rights movement condemned Black Power. Roy Wilkins was among its most virulent critics, calling it 'a reverse Mississippi, a reverse Hitler, a reverse Ku Klux Klan'. Although more muted in tone, A. Philip Randolph, Bayard Rustin and Whitney Young also rejected the slogan. Only CORE supported SNCC in its embrace of Black Power.

King sought to ease these divisions by exploiting Black Power's main weakness, which was also in many ways its greatest strength: its lack of any coherent meaning or programme. This rendered the Black Power slogan a powerfully emotive term that was endlessly open to both potentially positive and unifying, as well as potentially destructive and factionalizing, definitions and connotations.

In attempting to define Black Power, King recognized that the term had both 'assets and liabilities'. He acknowledged that Black Power was an understandable 'cry of disappointment' at how slow white America was to instigate change in response to black demands. He approved of Black Power's call 'to amass the political and economic strength' to achieve action on those demands. He understood Black Power's 'psychological call to manhood' after years of white domination and oppression.

Yet King also dismissed Black Power's embrace of hate and despair over love and hope, of armed self-defence and violence over non-violence, and of black nationalism and black separatism over integration and the forging of coalitions and allegiances with whites. These central tenets of the civil rights movement, King insisted, must remain to the fore as they had in the past if that movement was to continue to be successful.

King's efforts to paper over movement divisions about Black Power, however, were constantly undermined by Carmichael and others, who failed to refute the sensationalism and scaremongering of the white press over the slogan. This made sure that Black Power, Carmichael himself (whose penchant for self-publicity led some in the movement to label him 'Stokely Starmichael') and SNCC remained in the headlines [**Doc. 18, p. 150**].

Black Power proved a hit among young urban blacks with its message of community empowerment. It quickly spread from the rural South into US cities nationwide. Indeed, the formation of groups like the Black Panther Party by Bobby Seale and Huey Newton in Oakland, California, in 1966, with their quasi-militaristic black uniform and berets, insistence on bearing arms, and slogans like 'All power to the people!' became emblematic of the movement.

If Black Power did not mark the decisive end to the civil rights movement that James Forman claimed, then it did mark the beginning of the end. Over the following years, King would play his own part in closing that chapter of the black freedom struggle. His direct condemnation of US foreign policy in Vietnam, his support for and involvement in the growing anti-war movement, and his pursuit of a more radical economic agenda in the final years of his life, would change forever the civil rights movement as it had once existed.

Further reading

James Meredith, *Three Years in Mississippi* (1966) gives a first-hand account of his back-story. On his 1962 desegregation of the University of Mississippi see Charles W. Eagles, *The Price of Defiance: James Meredith and the Integration of Ole Miss* (2009). The best analysis of Black Power from the perspective of the times is Stokely Carmichael and Charles V. Hamilton, *Black Power: The Politics of Liberation in Black America* (1967). On Carmichael see Stokely Carmichael, with Eknueme Michael Thelwell, *Ready for Revolution: The Life and Struggles of Stokely Carmichael* [Kwame Ture] (2003). For many years, historians tended to neglect the Black Power movement. A recent flowering of new scholarship has corrected that. The best synthesis of this new scholarship is Peniel E. Joseph, *Waiting 'Til the Midnight Hour: A Narrative History of Black Power in America* (2007). Other notable works include Matthew Countryman, *Up South: Civil Rights and Black Power in Philadelphia* (2006); Lance Hill, *The Deacons for Defense: Armed Resistance and the Civil Rights Movement* (2004); Peniel E. Joseph, ed., *The Black Power Movement: Rethinking the Civil Rights–Black Power Era* (2006); Jeffrey O. G. Ogbar, *Black Power: Radical Politics and African American Identity* (2004); Timothy B. Tyson, *Radio Free Dixie: Robert F. Williams and the Roots of Black Power* (1999); and William L. Van Deburg, *New Day in Babylon: The Black Power Movement and American Culture, 1965–1975* (1992).

13

Civil Rights and the Vietnam War, 1965–1967

The United States' involvement in Vietnam dated back to the 1950s when it had supported the South Vietnam regime of President Ngo Dinh Diem as a Cold War imperative to prevent its takeover by communist North Vietnam under the leadership of Ho Chi Minh. Presidents Eisenhower, Kennedy and Johnson had all gradually committed more military personnel to bolster the South Vietnam regime. It was during President Johnson's second term in office from 1964 to 1968, however, that the first US combat soldiers were sent to Vietnam and a massive escalation of troops began. As the US became more heavily involved in and committed to the conflict, the Vietnam War, and growing public opposition to it, became one of the central issues of national concern.

Initially, King chose to stay silent about the war in Vietnam since he feared that linking the civil rights and anti-war issues would dilute the national impact of the civil rights movement. Moreover, taking an overt anti-war stance risked alienating key constituencies of movement support, not least President Johnson himself. Yet, as an advocate of non-violence and a man of conscience, it became increasingly difficult for King to remain silent.

Early in 1965 King began to tentatively speak out against the war. His first public utterance came in a speech at Howard University in Washington DC on 2 March 1965, when he told the audience that 'The war in Vietnam is accomplishing nothing.' By July 1965, King's statements on the war were becoming much bolder and were directly opposed to the Johnson administration's policy. As the SCLC conference approached in August 1965, King formulated a plan with his advisers to write to all of the principal countries involved in the Vietnam War to urge a negotiated settlement to the conflict.

However, when King met with the SCLC board, he found its normally compliant members unsettled by the plan. Although the board recognized King's right to speak out against the war as an individual, the SCLC reaffirmed that its primary goal was the pursuit of 'full citizenship rights for Negro citizens', and maintained that 'resources are not sufficient to assume the burden of two major issues'. King remained determined to pursue his letter-writing initiative, regardless of the board's reservations.

Further pressure for King to curtail his comments about the Vietnam War came from President Johnson. Johnson rebuked King over his public anti-war stance and initiated a meeting between King and Johnson's ambassador to the United Nations, Arthur Goldberg, with hopes of muting King's opposition. When King and Goldberg met, however, King continued to insist that the United States should work towards a negotiated settlement. In a further criticism of existing American foreign policy, King also suggested that the United States should drop its opposition to the People's Republic of China entering the United Nations.

The following day, Connecticut senator Thomas Dodd, a close ally of the Johnson administration, lambasted King's comments on Vietnam and 'Red China'. The pressure being exerted upon him by the Johnson administration prompted King to call another meeting with his advisers. At the meeting, King indicated a willingness to heed Johnson's warnings to backtrack and to mute his statements about the war. King told his advisers that he felt isolated and vulnerable in speaking out on Vietnam, and feared that his position as a civil rights leader would be undermined as a result. King's advisers agreed.

Although Dodd's comments effectively silenced King in the short term, the growing momentum of the anti-war movement inevitably brought King back to the issue. In January 1966, the Bond affair indicated that civil rights and anti-war issues were becoming ever more intertwined. The Georgia state legislature refused to seat the recently elected Julian Bond, former SNCC communications director, because he endorsed SNCC's view that people should take up civil rights work rather than submit to military draft. King leapt to Bond's defence, telling the press that 'in my current role as a pacifist I would be a conscientious objector'.

King led a rally to the Georgia state capitol in support of Bond, but King's comments to the press revealed that he still remained cautious about being drawn too far on the Vietnam question. King said that he supported SNCC's stand against the draft in principle but pointed out that he personally was not prepared to encourage breaking the law by draft dodging.

King's equivocation continued throughout 1966 as he studiously avoided participation in the burgeoning peace rallies and public discussions about the war. Yet he did not keep totally silent on the subject. In an awkward compromise, he often referred to the war indirectly by assessing its damaging impact on civil rights and anti-poverty efforts.

At its April 1966 convention, the SCLC adopted a resolution that 'The intense expectations and hopes of the neglected poor in the United States must be regarded as a priority more urgent than a conflict so rapidly degen-erating into a sordid military adventure.' At its August convention, the SCLC called for an immediate and unilateral de-escalation of the war, warning that it was 'corrupting American society from within and degrading it from without'. Invited to speak before the US Senate's Government Operations Committee in December 1966, King identified the war in Vietnam as one of the principal reasons for resources being drained away from anti-poverty efforts.

King's decisive turning point over Vietnam came in January 1967. As he was preparing to fly to Jamaica to work on his latest book he came across an article by William Pepper in *Ramparts* magazine about 'The Children of Vietnam'. The article discussed and graphically illustrated the horrific injuries inflicted in Vietnam by the United States' use of chemical weapons such as napalm.

While King was in Jamaica, James Bevel visited to ask for another leave of absence from the SCLC, this time to become national director of the anti-war **Spring Mobilization** Committee, which was planning a mass demonstration in New York City. Bevel urged King to join the demonstration and to speak out more forthrightly against the war. Other SCLC staff members Harry Boyte, John Barber and Robert Green, along with former SCLC staff member James Lawson, were also active in helping to organize anti-war rallies.

Spring Mobilization: A 1967 movement de-signed to bring together anti-war supporters in a push to withdraw US troops from Vietnam.

When King returned from Jamaica, he indicated that he was finally ready to tie 'the peace movement to the civil rights movement or vice-versa', even if that meant an explicit break with the Johnson administration. At a 25 February speech in Los Angeles, King roundly condemned the 'triple evils of racism, extreme materialism and militarism', while criticizing American for-eign policy in Vietnam, which, he insisted, represented 'white colonialism', 'paranoid anti-communism' and 'deadly western arrogance'.

Most of King's SCLC advisers remained adamantly opposed to his par-ticipation in the Spring Mobilization, scheduled for 15 April 1967, believing that his participation would mean a total and decisive breakdown in the civil rights movement's relationship with the Johnson administration. King nevertheless decided to take part. On 25 March, he led his first anti-war march of 5,000 people in Chicago, alongside noted paediatrician and anti-war spokesperson Dr Benjamin Spock.

Ultimately, however, it was not King's participation in the Spring Mobilization that grabbed the headlines, but rather his speech at New York's Riverside Church on 4 April, delivered to the group Clergy and Laymen Concerned about Vietnam [**Doc. 19, p. 152**]. Drafted with the help of black historian Vincent Harding, King's speech contained his harshest condemnation yet of the Vietnam War and of the Johnson administration. Denouncing the United States as 'the greatest purveyor of violence in the world today', King demanded that the US halt its bombing of Vietnam, declare a unilateral ceasefire, curtail its

forces in Thailand and Laos, accept Viet Cong representation in peace negotiations, and set a date for the withdrawal of US troops [**Doc. 19, p. 152**].

Reaction to King's speech was far more negative than he had anticipated.
On 6 April, the *Washington Post* summed up the prevailing sentiment when
it announced that King 'has done a grave injury to those who are his natural
allies . . . Many who have listened to him with respect will never again accord
him the same confidence.' *Life* magazine called the speech 'a demagogic
slander that sounded like a script for [North Vietnamese] Radio Hanoi'. John
P. Roche, special assistant to the President, told Johnson in a memo that
'King . . . has thrown in with the communists' and 'is destroying his reputation as a Negro leader'. Black columnist Carl T. Rowan bemoaned 'Martin
Luther King's Tragic Decision' to speak out on Vietnam in America's most
widely read magazine, *Readers Digest*.

Only a few newspapers and magazines backed King's statement, most
notably the *Christian Century*, which called his speech 'a magnificent blend of
eloquence and raw fact, of searing denunciation and tender wooing, of political
sagacity and Christian insight, of tough realism and infinite compassion'.

Within the civil rights movement, the NAACP's Roy Wilkins and National
Urban League's Whitney Young both distanced themselves from King's anti-
war stance. The NAACP board of directors warned that attempts to merge
civil rights and anti-war movements would be a 'serious tactical mistake'.
A. Philip Randolph and Bayard Rustin both refused to comment on King's
speech to the press. Later, however, Rustin wrote an article in New York's
Amsterdam News on 'Dr. King's Painful Dilemma', in which he noted that 'the
involvement of the civil rights organizations as such in peace activities' was
'unprofitable and perhaps even suicidal'.

King conceded that the speech may have been 'politically unwise', but at
the same time insisted that it was 'morally wise'. For FBI director J. Edgar
Hoover, King's speech was grist to the mill for his allegations about subversive communist influence on the civil rights leader. President Johnson
was now far more disposed to agree with Hoover's analysis.

King remained unrepentant in the face of public criticism. Appearing on
the Columbia Broadcasting System (CBS) *Face the Nation* television programme
on 16 April, King insisted that the civil rights and anti-war movements were
indeed tied together 'from a content point of view, although the two are not
joined together from an organizational point of view'. King encouraged
potential army draftees to apply for conscientious objector status, although
he was opposed to breaking federal law through draft evasion.

On 23 April, King joined Dr Benjamin Spock to announce plans for a
'Vietnam Summer' in conjunction with Clergy and Laymen Concerned about
Vietnam. With more than a passing resemblance to SNCC's 1964 Freedom
Summer in Mississippi, 'Vietnam Summer' proposed to mobilize grassroots

opposition to the war into a nationwide network. The next day, King joined a new peace group called 'Negotiation Now'. On 25 April, King, alongside James Bevel, Dr Benjamin Spock, and Harry Belafonte, led a peace march of 125,000 from New York's Central Park to United Nations Plaza.

King's anti-war stance even began to filter through into his sermons at Ebenezer Baptist Church, where he praised black boxer Muhammed Ali's refusal to enlist in the US army to fight in Vietnam. King's name was even mentioned as a potential third party peace candidate for the 1968 presidential election. Meanwhile, polls suggested that, as many of King's advisers had feared, much of the black community did not share his anti-war stance. According to one opinion poll, only a quarter of blacks backed him over the issue.

King nevertheless remained optimistic about tying together civil rights and anti-war sentiment, possibly by mobilizing another March on Washington type event. However, over the summer of 1967, the impetus of the Spring Mobilization began to fade. A short-lived Arab–Israeli war broke out in June that eclipsed the war in Vietnam in the national news headlines. The Middle East conflict muted much of the anti-war movement's liberal Jewish supporters, one of the movement's key constituencies. Israel's use of military might to resolve the conflict held out the promise that the United States' continuing use of force in Vietnam might bring about a similar victory. While these developments robbed the anti-war movement of momentum and publicity, the movement itself became increasingly fractious. By the end of the summer, the anti-war movement was left in disarray and appeared a spent force.

A new outbreak of ghetto riots during July and August in Newark, New Jersey, and Detroit, Michigan, had also diverted attention away from the war. President Johnson set up a **National Advisory Commission on Civil Disorders**, which became known as the Kerner Commission, named after its chair, Governor Otto Kerner of Illinios. The report that the commission produced, published in February 1968, was damning of US race relations, laying much of the blame for the rioting on white racism and the reporting of the white media. It blamed poor housing, poor education, poor social services, and high unemployment as sources of the riots [**Doc. 20, p. 152**]. Its sobering conclusion, for the civil rights movement and for America, was that 'Our nation is moving toward two societies, one black, one white – separate and unequal.'

National Advisory Commission on Civil Disorders: Also known as the Kerner Commission after its chair Illinois governor Otto Kerner, the commission investigated the causes of the 'long hot summers' of racial unrest between 1965 and 1967.

Further reading

A good starting point for an overview of King's final years is Thomas F. Jackson, *From Civil Rights to Human Rights: Martin Luther King, Jr. and the Struggle for Economic Justice* (2007). On King and Vietnam, about which relatively little has been written, see Herbert Aptheker, *Dr. Martin Luther*

King, Vietnam and Civil Rights (1967), Adam Fairclough, 'Martin Luther King, Jr. and the War in Vietnam', *Phylon* 45 (1984): 19–39, and Taylor Branch, *At Canaan's Edge: America in the King Years, 1965–68* (2006). On the wider connections between the civil rights and anti-war movements see Simon Hall, *Peace and Freedom: The Civil Rights and the Antiwar Movements in the 1960s* (2005).

14

The Poor People's Campaign and Memphis, 1967–1968

In mid-September 1967, King arranged an SCLC retreat in Warrenton, Virginia, to discuss an idea put to him by Marian Wright, an NAACP attorney working in Mississippi. Wright's suggestion was to take the crippling poverty she had witnessed in Mississippi to the seat of power in Washington DC to dramatize the plight of the black poor. Her initial suggestion was to stage a sit-in at the national headquarters of the Office of Heath, Education and Welfare.

Expanding upon this idea, King suggested a more ambitious campaign. He proposed a march of several thousand volunteers to Washington DC to occupy the city and hold a concerted campaign of 'civil disobedience'. This would involve a significant upscaling of non-violent direct action to another level, expressly aimed at disrupting the normal day-to-day running of the nation's capital, with demands for 'jobs and income' for the poor.

Between 27 November and 1 December the SCLC held another retreat to discuss progress on the Poor People's Campaign (PPC), as it had become known. King articulated an even more radical vision of how the PPC might unfold. He told SCLC staff that they had underestimated just how entrenched racism was in the United States. The gains made between 1955 and 1965 had barely scratched the surface, he said. The true challenge they now faced was 'bring[ing] the social change movements through from their early and now inadequate protest phase to a stage of massive, active, nonviolent resistance to the evils of the modern system'.

This could be achieved, King said, through building a coalition of the poor and oppressed, not just including blacks, but also 'Puerto Ricans, Mexicans, Indians from the reservations, and poor whites from Appalachia'. Initial goals would involve securing employment opportunities and a minimum income level, and include demands for an elimination of the slums. Andrew

Young, promoted to SCLC executive vice-president, suggested that the movement might employ tactics such as 'lying on highways, blocking doors at government offices, and mass school boycotts'.

This campaign of disruption would culminate in another March on Washington. However, this time the demonstration would not last for just one day but would instead occupy the nation's capital indefinitely until the Johnson administration was forced to reassess its domestic and foreign policy. At the end of the retreat on 4 December, King informed the press that the campaign would begin in April.

During November and December 1967 the Canadian Broadcasting Corporation aired a series of talks that King had recorded earlier that year. They revealed more about King's thoughts on the PPC. King insisted that 'Nonviolent protest must now mature to a new level to correspond to heightened black impatience and stiffened white reaction. This higher level is mass civil disobedience.' This new departure would offer an antidote to recent black violence, King said, and 'transmute the deep rage of the ghetto into a constructive and creative force'. The PPC would comprise 'a sustained, massive, direct action movement in Washington', offering 'a new economic deal for the poor'.

The talks revealed that alongside a nationalization of demonstrations, King was also contemplating an agenda for the internationalization of non-violent direct action. 'Can a nonviolent, direct action movement find application on the international level, to confront economic and political problems?' King asked. 'I believe it can. It is clear to me that the next stage in the movement is to become international.'

King hinted at just how wide-ranging this internationalization might be, and how it was tied to the new economic focus of the civil rights movement. 'We in the West must bear in mind that poor countries are poor primarily because we have exploited them through political or economic colonialism,' King told listeners. 'Americans in particular must help their nation repent of her modern economic imperialism.'

King's comments encompassed global issues from South America – 'So many of Latin America's problem's have roots in the United States of America' – to South Africa – 'If just two countries, Britain and the United States, could be persuaded to end all economic interaction with the South African regime, they could bring that government to its knees in a relatively short space of time.' Overall, King's ambition appeared to be nothing short of an effort 'to planetize our movement for racial justice'.

Despite King's apparent optimism, doubts about the over-ambition and viability of the PPC remained within the SCLC. King's opponents were predictably even more adamantly opposed. President Johnson berated the campaign and urged the civil rights movement to use its energies more productively. Congress explored the possibility of banning all demonstrations in the nation's capital. The FBI further intensified its campaign against the civil rights movement.

King defended his plans to movement supporters and to political opponents. He insisted that the indistinct goals of the PPC were strengths rather than weaknesses. King contended that the campaign needed a simple slogan of 'jobs and income' that people could rally around and not complicated and detailed policy programmes. He pointed out that previous campaigns in Montgomery, Birmingham and Selma had not had detailed blueprints. Rather, mobilization had occurred first and the precise details had been worked out after the momentum of demonstrations had been established. The same would be true of the PPC.

By March 1968, the indications were that the PPC was beginning to take shape. The recruitment quotas of people for each targeted area in the country had not only been achieved but exceeded. Donations through the SCLC's direct mailing programme were beginning to pick up. Labour unions, religious organizations and other interracial groups were starting to lend their support. Nevertheless, as Andrew Young admitted, 'We still hadn't worked out the details.'

Just as the PPC seemed to be gathering momentum, King was sidetracked by an escalating union dispute in Memphis, Tennessee. The 1,300-strong members of the predominantly black **American Federation of State, County and Municipal Employees (AFSCME)** had been on strike since 12 February, angered at unfair treatment of its members and at the refusal of city officials to negotiate over a union dues 'checkoff' system. The checkoff system meant that dues were deducted straight from pay packets, which ensured regular union contributions. Without it, already lowly paid workers were often reluctant to relinquish dues on payday.

American Federation of State, County and Municipal Employees: Labour union that represents local and state government employees.

Memphis mayor Henry Loeb refused to recognize the union at all, let alone the validity of its complaints. Attempts to broker a compromise by white union leaders, the Memphis Ministers Association, and national AFSCME president Jerry Wurf, all failed. On 23 February the conflict escalated further when city police employed Mace, tear gas and billyclubs to break up a union march. In the mêlée, participating black ministers and federal observers were also gassed.

The actions of the city police helped to galvanize support for the striking workers and the following day 150 blacks, half of them ministers, formed **Community on the Move for Equality (COME)** to coordinate black community support for the strike. To exert pressure on the city, COME launched a boycott of downtown stores and white newspapers, and organized daily movement marches and evening rallies. When the city still refused to budge, COME sought to attract national support for its cause.

Community on the Move for Equality: A Memphis coalition of striking workers and ministers formed to support the sanitation workers' strike.

King's old friend James Lawson, a minister in Memphis and a member of COME, requested King's support. When he arrived in Memphis on 18 March, King addressed an enthusiastic crowd of 15,000 people at Mason Temple. He later told black Memphis minister Billy Kyles that he had detected 'that old movement spirit' that night, and that the strike might be the beginning of a 'rejuvenation of the movement'.

So moved was King by the response that he told the crowd, 'In a few days you ought to get together and just have a general work stoppage in the city of Memphis', to allow all blacks in the city to show solidarity with the striking workers and to put more pressure on city officials to negotiate.

After conferring with Lawson, King announced that he would return to Memphis on the day of the general strike, which was scheduled for 22 March. Recognizing that the dispute highlighted the intertwined nature of racial justice and economic power, King specifically tied the situation in Memphis to the PPC by announcing that the one-day general strike would mark 'the beginning of the Washington movement [the PPC]'.

The one-day strike in Memphis had to be rescheduled for 28 March after a heavy snowfall disrupted plans for the 22nd. When King flew into Memphis on 28 March, his flight was delayed, meaning that those who had assembled at Clayborn Temple AME Church were kept waiting for over an hour for the march in support of the strike to begin.

The delay proved to be a fateful one. As they waited, the crowd grew restless and impatient. Usually, marches headed by King and the SCLC took place only after careful preparation and training in non-violence. Organization of the Memphis march was left in the hands of local black leaders who made only perfunctory preparations for it. Among the milling crowd were members of a local Black Power group, the Black Organizing Project, or the 'Invaders', who had been left out of discussions about the march. Alongside the Invaders there were, one student on the march noted, 'fellows sitting around drinking wine and beer and waiting for the march to begin. They began talking about looting stores.'

When King, Ralph Abernathy, and other SCLC staff members finally arrived, they were unaware of the potentially volatile mix. There were warning signs of the unruliness of the crowd when King's arrival was greeted by a disorganized crush. Lawson suggested delaying the march further to address the problem, but SCLC staff dismissed his entreaties, mistaking the uneasy mood of the crowd for exuberance and enthusiasm. 'We've been in this kind of situation before,' they told Lawson. 'There's a lot of excitement in the beginning, but if we hold on and go on, the march will get itself straightened out and everything will be all right.'

However, it did not take long for the march to descend into chaos. The crowd remained unruly. As the marchers turned into Main Street, white attorney Walter Bailey 'saw a group of young punks with sticks hitting a pawn shop window, and I said to myself "Good heavens! What the hell are they trying to do? Get us all shot?"' Cries of 'Smash glass' and 'Burn it down, baby' could be heard as looting broke out. The march had lasted less than half an hour.

At the outbreak of looting, Lawson took the decision to disband. 'This is Rev. Lawson speaking,' he said, using a borrowed police bullhorn. 'I want everyone who's in the march, in the Movement, to turn back around and go back to church.' Before the retreat got under way, however, city police waded into the crowd and used Mace and tear gas to break up the demonstration. King had already been ushered away by his aides. The day's events led to 282 arrests, 62 injuries, and the death of 17-year-old Larry Payne, who was shot by a Memphis police officer. A 7.00 p.m. curfew was imposed, enforced by 3,800 members of the Tennessee National Guard.

Back at King's hotel, infuriated aides demanded to know why COME leaders had allowed King to step into such a badly organized and badly planned march. King was extremely subdued. 'Never have I led a march where the demonstrators committed acts of violence,' he told Abernathy, adding, 'Maybe we'll just have to let violence have its chance.' Yet clearly another peaceful march was an absolute necessity. Since King had explicitly linked the situation in Memphis to the PPC, the whole Washington DC campaign now hinged upon King's ability to show that he could still hold a disciplined, non-violent demonstration, without it descending into violence.

The next morning, three leaders of the Black Power group the Invaders, Charles Cabbage, Calvin Taylor and Charles Harrington, arrived at King's hotel room: King agreed to see them. 'What can I do . . . to have a peaceful march?' he asked them, 'Because you know that I have to lead one.' The Invaders indicated that in return for financial help for their community organizing plans they would cooperate with another march. However, they still insisted that they could not wholly guarantee a peaceful passage.

King explained that the SCLC did not have the money to fund the Invaders project but he agreed to make enquiries elsewhere on their behalf. Later, King told the press that the SCLC had not played a role in the organization of the march the previous day but that it would take responsibility for running a second, peaceful march through the city.

In public, King confidently asserted that the situation in Memphis, which demonstrated the link between issues of race and class, underlined exactly why the PPC was necessary and insisted that it would still go ahead. In private, he was far more doubtful, telling Abernathy, 'Ralph, I want to get out of Memphis. Get me out of Memphis as soon as possible.'

A meeting with the SCLC's executive staff back in Atlanta was arranged to discuss developments. When King outlined plans for a second Memphis march as a way of getting the PPC back on track, it inspired little enthusiasm. After facing several hours of dissent, King stood up and announced that he was leaving the meeting and that they could probably sort out the organization's problems better without him. As one of the young dissenters, Jesse Jackson, followed King to the door, King launched an uncharacteristically personal attack on him, saying 'Jesse, it may be necessary for you to carve out your own individual niche in society. But you don't bother me.'

Staff discussions continued without King. After a gruelling ten hours of debate, they agreed to back another march. SCLC staff James Orange, Jesse Jackson, James Bevel and Hosea Williams were sent to Memphis to pave the way for a second march scheduled for 5 April. Orange took on the nettlesome task of reconciling local Memphis factions the Invaders and COME. Though a great deal of personal antipathy remained on both sides, Orange got the two organizations to agree to work together on the forthcoming march, rescheduled for 8 April.

King travelled to Washington DC to keep a prearranged engagement and returned to Atlanta for a couple of days before heading to Memphis on 3 April. As he participated in a meeting at James Lawson's church, news came through that Federal District judge Bailey Brown had issued a restraining order against King and the SCLC. Six Memphis attorneys agreed to help fight the order on SCLC's behalf. King indicated that he intended to go ahead with the march whether the injunction was lifted or not.

The attorneys meanwhile devised a strategy whereby they would ask for a modification of the injunction to allow a small, disciplined group to hold a limited downtown march. This would strike a note of compromise with the court while at the same time heightening the chances of the march passing off without violence.

That evening, King was due to speak to a mass meeting at Mason Temple. However, exhausted, he sent Ralph Abernathy to deputize for him. Only 2,000 people turned up due to the stormy weather. Yet Abernathy sensed that those who had made the effort to get there were disappointed not to see King in person. Abernathy called King and told him, 'Martin, you know I would not ask you to come ordinarily, but these people want to hear you, and they want to see you.'

King agreed to go. His apparent weariness added to the emotional intensity of his speech. Part of the address dwelt on the time that he had been stabbed and had stared death in the face. If he had merely sneezed, King told the crowd, the blade might have pierced his heart and killed him. But he had not sneezed and he had gone on to see the great achievements of the movement through the sit-ins, the Freedom Rides, the March on Washington, and SCLC campaigns in Albany, Birmingham and Selma. There were difficult days ahead, King told them, 'But it really doesn't matter with me now, because

I've been to the mountaintop . . . and I've seen the promised land. I may not get there with you. But I want you to know tonight, that we, as a people will get to the promised land. And so I'm happy tonight. I'm not worried about anything. I'm not fearing any man. Mine eyes have see the glory of the coming of the Lord [His truth is marching on!].' [Doc. 21, p. 154]

The next day, 4 April, King did not wake until noon, by which time Andrew Young and James Lawson had already headed off to the district court with movement attorneys in an attempt to get Judge Bailey to modify the injunction against the planned march. King waited anxiously for news in his hotel room throughout the afternoon while discussing the continuing problems posed by the unpredictable Invaders with SCLC staff.

Later, Andrew Young and SCLC attorney Chauncey Eskridge returned from the court with the good news that the judge had agreed to their proposal for a scaled-down march the following Monday. King was in good humour at hearing the news and teased Young about his prolonged absence. Abernathy joined in the teasing and the three of them ended up in a pillow fight in a brief release from the tension-filled past few weeks.

Memphis minister Billy Kyles had invited King and his aides for a soul food supper that evening. With the time approaching 6.00 p.m. they began to ready themselves. Shortly afterwards, Kyles called to collect them. King walked out onto his second floor balcony at the Lorraine Motel beside Kyles, with driver Solomon Jones, Jr., and Andrew Young, Chauncey Eskridge, James Bevel, Jesse Jackson and Hosea Williams waiting for them in the courtyard below. Abernathy was still inside the hotel room fussing about and getting ready. Jones called up to King to put on a topcoat since it was getting cold. King sent Kyles on ahead while he went to get his coat from the room.

Suddenly, a single rifle shot rang out hitting King in the cheek. Abernathy rushed out of the room and Kyles and the others headed to the balcony. When Andrew Young reached King he was laid out on the balcony floor. Young looked over at Abernathy and cried 'Oh, my God, my God, it's all over, it's all over.' King was rushed to a Memphis hospital, but he was pronounced dead not long after arrival.

Further reading

On events in Memphis see Joan Turner Biefuss, *At the River I Stand: Memphis, the 1968 Strike, and Martin Luther King* (1985); G. Wayne Dowdy, *Crusades for Freedom: Memphis and the Political Transformation of the American South* (2010); Laurie B. Green, *Battling the Plantation Mentality: Memphis and the Black Freedom Struggle* (2007); and Michael K. Honey, *Going Down Jericho Road: The Memphis Strike, Martin Luther King's Last Campaign* (2007). On the Poor People's Campaign see Ronald L. Freeman, *The Mule Train: A*

Journey of Hope Remembered (1998); Hilliard Lawrence Lackey, *Marks, Martin and the Mule Train* (1998); and Gerald D. McKnight, *The Last Crusade: Martin Luther King Jr., the FBI, and the Poor People's Campaign* (1998).

King's assassination, like many others, has drawn many theories. Those who allege some form of conspiracy, collusion or cover-up include Mark Lane and Dick Gregory, *Murder in Memphis: The FBI and the Assassination of Martin Luther King* (1993) and William F. Pepper, *An Act of State: The Execution of Martin Luther King* (2003). The 'lone gunman' thesis is stated in Gerald Posner, *Killing the Dream: James Earl Ray and the Assassination of Martin Luther King, Jr.* (1998). King's alleged assassin wrote his own account before his 1998 death in jail in, James Earl Ray, *Who Killed Martin Luther King, Jr.?: The True Story by the Alleged Assassin* (1992). Recent works in the never-ending genre include Hampton Sides, *Hellhound on his Trail: The Stalking of Martin Luther King, Jr. and the International Hunt for his Assassin* (2010) and Stuart Wexler and Larry Hancock, *The Awful Grace of God: Religious Terrorism, White Supremacy, and the Unsolved Murder of Martin Luther King, Jr.* (2012).

Conclusion: Martin Luther King, Jr., the Civil Rights Movement, and the Black Freedom Struggle

Although the civil rights movement had been in decline for several years, no one single event signalled a decisive end to it more than King's assassination. Much of white America felt sympathy and remorse at King's death. President Johnson ordered flags to be flown at half-mast and declared the following Sunday a national day of mourning. In Memphis, on 5 April, 300 black and white ministers marched on City Hall. Eleven days later the city capitulated to the demands of the striking sanitation workers.

On 10 April, Congress passed the 1968 Civil Rights Act, although its provisions for fair housing and for the protection of civil rights workers had little practical impact. More white money poured into SCLC coffers than ever before. Yet in black America, King's death was greeted with anger and violence. Racial disturbances rocked more than 130 cities in 29 states, resulting in 46 deaths, over 7,000 injuries and 20,000 arrests, with damage to property estimated at over $100 million.

Although the outbreak of such violence might seem paradoxical, given King's commitment to non-violence, in fact it made every sense. King had maintained throughout his life that non-violence was the most viable antidote to violence. Blacks viewed King's death as white America's final rejection of non-violence and, just as King had predicted, turned decisively to violence instead. Black Power advocate Stokely Carmichael asserted that 'when white America killed Dr. King, she declared war on us . . . Black people have to survive, and the only way they will survive is by getting a gun.'

As King had also predicted, the use of black violence only brought greater white counter-violence. The federal government ruthlessly suppressed and quickly crushed a black militant insurgency within a few short years. Without

King, the SCLC's influence quickly melted away. Ralph Abernathy took over as president of the organization and presided over an ill-fated Poor People's Campaign that failed to win any significant concessions. Shortly afterwards, many of the influential members of the SCLC during King's lifetime left the organization, which had become riddled with factionalism and disagreements in King's absence.

As events unfolded after King's death, they underscored just what his presence had meant to the civil rights movement. 'Ultimately,' King once reflected, 'a genuine leader is not a searcher for consensus but a molder of consensus.' As president of the SCLC, King had acted as a lightning rod to attract a cadre of talented local black southern leaders. King had kept conflicting egos within the SCLC largely at bay during his lifetime. Never resorting to autocratic leadership, King allowed SCLC staff members a great deal of leeway to develop new ideas and tactics, while reining in their over-ambition and cautioning against excess.

King's leadership of the SCLC was in many ways a microcosm of his leadership role in the civil rights movement. As part of what was an often fractious and factious movement, King commanded more respect and trust in more sections of the black community than any other black leader of the time.

Central to King's ability to achieve this respect and trust was his grounding in the black southern Baptist church tradition. King used the black church as a spiritual and organizational base for the movement. He tapped the latent religious sentiment and fervour of the black church while using his position at the head of a key black community institution to appeal to more secular sections of the black community as well.

King made the idea of non-violence and the tactic of non-violent direct action appear like a seamless extension of the black church and black religion. Yet in fact, in employing non-violent direct action tactics, King managed to combine what was often a very conservative black community institution with a far more radical tradition of non-violence developed by pacifists and socialists on the American political left. In this way, he was able to appeal to both conservative and militant wings of the movement. As historian and activist August Meier has noted, King could very well be described as a 'conservative militant'.

King effectively acted as a bridge between different sections of the black community. In a decade when American youth implored their generation not to trust anyone over 30, King turned 31 in January 1960. This placed him on the cusp of being young enough to relate to influential student demonstrators, but mature and respected enough to mediate between them and older and more conservative black leaders such as the NAACP's Roy Wilkins and the NUL's Whitney Young.

King also used his status and authority as a black minister to successfully appeal to both the 'classes' and the 'masses', or, as King put it, 'the PhDs and the no "Ds"' in the southern black community. Of course, King could not appeal to everyone all of the time. Many black northerners did not identify with his distinctly southern and religious sensibilities. As the civil rights movement became more fractious after 1965, King often found himself stranded in the middle ground – too old, too conservative, and too bourgeois for a new generation of younger, working-class-oriented black militants, yet too young and too radical for older, more conservative middle-class black leaders.

Just as important as King's ability to unite the black community was his ability to reach out to large sections of America's white community and to engage them in the civil rights movement. Non-violent direct action high-lighted the inconsistency of brutal southern enforcement of segregation and disenfranchisement with white America's claims to be a fundamentally democratic and moral society. The tactic therefore appealed to white liberals on the very grounds that they were most likely to listen to and to make con-cessions on.

King also had the ability to verbally articulate the demands of the black community in a way that both blacks and whites could identify with and understand. Combining his experience as an orator in the black folk pulpit tradition with ideas, rhetoric and values imbibed in his northern white liberal seminary and university education, King skilfully fused texts such as the Bible with the Constitution and the Declaration of Independence to pro-vide a vision of social and racial justice which merged, as historian Rosemary R. Ruether notes, 'prophetic Christianity and the American civic creed'. Black writer James Baldwin was not the only one to note that 'King's secret lay in the intimate knowledge of his audience, black or white, and in the forthright-ness with which he spoke of the things that hurt or baffled them.'

The most enduring markers of King's success as leader of the civil rights movement are the 1964 Civil Rights Act and the 1965 Voting Rights Act. The 1964 Civil Rights Act was passed in a climate for racial reform created by King and the SCLC's 1963 Birmingham Campaign and the 1963 March on Washington, and was speeded by the grief over the assassination of President Kennedy and by the political skill and commitment to civil rights of his successor, President Johnson. The act ended the practice of legalized segrega-tion in the South that had provided a highly visible, day-to-day enforcement of black social inferiority.

The 1965 Voting Rights Act was passed as a direct consequence of King and the SCLC's 1965 Selma Campaign and opened up a path for blacks to join the southern body politic and to begin in earnest the process of building black political power. The 1965 Voting Rights Act meant that far larger numbers of southern blacks were able to vote without impediment. It also meant that blacks could actually run for election to positions such as president, US Congress, state congress, governor, and mayor, as well as for election to positions such as local judge, local sheriff, and local school board member, with a far more realistic chance of success.

An integral part of the civil rights movement was also a transformation in black self-awareness, self-confidence and self-respect. Participation in the movement enabled many blacks to stand shoulder to shoulder in opposition to white oppression and in the process to overcome their fear of white violence and intimidation. The movement proved psychologically, as well as legally and politically, liberating.

However, not all of King's and the movement's endeavours were successful. King's efforts to focus on economic issues during his final years were only at an embryonic stage at the time of his death and he never achieved the kind of far-reaching redistribution of wealth that he sought.

Ultimately, King and the civil rights movement helped blacks to gain access to and build a platform for social and political power. In doing so, they fostered a sense of black empowerment and psychological liberation that provided the foundations for implementing and for furthering those gains. Yet King and the civil rights movement barely had a chance to begin the much bigger and far more complex task of translating notional rights under the law into actual social, political and economic power. That new phase of the struggle for black freedom and equality succeeded King and the movement and continues today.

Part 6

DOCUMENTS

Document 1   THIRTEENTH AMENDMENT TO THE US CONSTITUTION, 1865

The Thirteenth Amendment abolished slavery, the first step for black Americans on the road to freedom and equality.

Section 1. Neither slavery nor involuntary servitude, except as a punishment for crime whereof the party shall have been duly convicted, shall exist within the United States, or any place subject to their jurisdiction.

Document 2   FOURTEENTH AMENDMENT TO THE US CONSTITUTION, 1868

The Fourteenth Amendment defined what it meant to be a citizen of the US – 'born or naturalized' – and promised equal protection of the laws to all citizens.

Section 1. All persons born or naturalized in the United States and subject to the jurisdiction thereof, are citizens of the United States and of the State wherein they reside. No State shall make or enforce any law which shall abridge the privileges or immunities of citizens of the United States; nor shall any State deprive any person of life, liberty, or property, without due process of law; nor deny to any person within its jurisdiction the equal protection of the laws.

Document 3   FIFTEENTH AMENDMENT TO THE US CONSTITUTION, 1870

The Fifteenth Amendment promised voting rights to all male citizens Women did not get the vote until the adoption of the Nineteenth Amendment in 1920.

Section 1. The right of citizens of the United States to vote shall not be denied or abridged by the United States or by any State on account of race, color, or previous condition of servitude.

Document 4   *BROWN V. BOARD OF EDUCATION*, 17 MAY 1954

*The **Brown** decision outlawed segregation in schools and undermined the notion of 'separate but equal'. In reversing its earlier decision, the Court pointed to the changed context of education in American society since **Plessy** and to new psychological evidence about the impact of segregation on schoolchildren.*

MR. CHIEF JUSTICE WARREN delivered the opinion of the Court . . .

In approaching this problem, we cannot turn the clock back to 1868, when the Amendment was adopted, or even to 1896, when Plessy v. Ferguson was written. We must consider public education in the light of its full development and its present place in American life throughout the Nation. Only in this way can it be determined if segregation in public schools deprives these plaintiffs of the equal protection of the laws.

Today, education is perhaps the most important function of state and local governments. Compulsory school attendance laws and the great expenditures for education both demonstrate our recognition of the importance of education to our democratic society. It is required in the performance of our most basic public responsibilities, even service in the armed forces. It is the very foundation of good citizenship. Today it is a principal instrument in awakening the child to cultural values, in preparing him for later professional training, and in helping him to adjust normally to his environment. In these days, it is doubtful that any child may reasonably be expected to succeed in life if he is denied the opportunity of an education. Such an opportunity, where the state has undertaken to provide it, is a right which must be made available to all on equal terms.

We come then to the question presented: Does segregation of children in public schools solely on the basis of race, even though the physical facilities and other 'tangible' factors may be equal, deprive the children of the minority group of equal educational opportunities? We believe that it does . . .

Segregation of white and colored children in public schools has a detrimental effect upon the colored children. The impact is greater when it has the sanction of the law, for the policy of separating the races is usually interpreted as denoting the inferiority of the negro group. A sense of inferiority affects the motivation of a child to learn. Segregation with the sanction of law, therefore, has a tendency to [retard] the educational and mental development of negro children and to deprive them of some of the benefits they would receive in a racial[ly] integrated school system.

Whatever may have been the extent of psychological knowledge at the time of Plessy v. Ferguson, this finding is amply supported by modern authority. Any language in Plessy v. Ferguson contrary to this finding is rejected.

We conclude that, in the field of public education, the doctrine of 'separate but equal' has no place. Separate educational facilities are inherently unequal. Therefore, we hold that the plaintiffs and others similarly situated for whom the actions have been brought are, by reason of the segregation complained of, deprived of the equal protection of the laws guaranteed by the Fourteenth Amendment.

Source: http://www.nationalcenter.org/brown.html

Document 5   MARTIN LUTHER KING, JR., 'AUTOBIOGRAPHY OF RELIGIOUS
DEVELOPMENT', 1950

*A 21-year-old King gives a candid and revealing insight into his early life
and religious development in this class paper written at Crozer Theological
Seminary in Chester, Pennsylvania.*

Source: http://stanford.edu/group/King/publications/papers/vol1/501122-An_Auto-
biography_of_Religious_Development.htm

Document 6   A LETTER FROM THE WOMEN'S POLITICAL COUNCIL TO THE MAYOR OF
MONTGOMERY, ALABAMA, 21 MAY 1954

*Jo Ann Robinson's letter to Mayor Gayle, sent over a year before the
Montgomery bus boycott began, tells us at least three things. Firstly, treatment of blacks on buses was an ongoing issue in Montgomery. Secondly,
as was the case at the outset of the boycott, blacks pressed for modification
of segregation, not its complete abolition. Thirdly, the impact of* Brown *on
emboldening black demands – the letter was written just four days after the
Court ruling.*

> Honorable Mayor W. Gayle
> City Hall
> Montgomery, Alabama
>
> Dear Sir:
> The Women's Political Council is very grateful to you and the City
> Commissioners for the hearing you allowed our representative during the
> month of March, 1954, when the 'city-bus-fare-increase case' was being
> reviewed. There were several things the Council asked for:
>
> 1. A city law that would make it possible for Negroes to sit from back toward
>   front, and whites from front toward back until all the seats are taken.
> 2. That Negroes not be asked or forced to pay fare at front and go to the
>   rear of the bus to enter.
> 3. That busses stop at every corner in residential sections occupied by
>   Negroes as they do in communities where whites reside.
>
> We are happy to report that busses have begun stopping at more corners
> now in some sections where Negroes live than previously. However, the
> same practices in seating and boarding the bus continue.
>   Mayor Gayle, three-fourths of the riders of these public conveyances are
> Negroes. If Negroes did not patronize them, they could not possibly operate.

County, four of the people got off to use the washroom, and two of the people
– to use the restaurant – two of the people wanted to use the washroom.

The four people that had gone in to use the restaurant was ordered out.
During this time I was on the bus. But when I looked through the window
and saw they had rushed out I got off of the bus to see what had happened.
And one of the ladies said, 'It was a State Highway Patrolman and a Chief of
Police ordered us out.'

I got back on the bus and one of the persons had used the washroom got
back on the bus, too.

As soon as I was seated on the bus, I saw when they began to get the five
people in a highway patrolman's car. I stepped off of the bus to see what was
happening and somebody screamed from the car that the five workers was
in and said, 'Get that one there.' And when I went to get in the car, when the
man told me I was under arrest, he kicked me.

I was carried to the county jail and put in the booking room. They left
some of the people in the booking room and began to place us in cells. I was
placed in a cell with a young woman called Miss Ivesta Simpson. After I was
placed in the cell I began to hear sounds of licks and screams. I could hear
the sounds of licks and horrible screams. And I could hear somebody say,
'Can you say, "yes, sir," nigger? Can you say "yes, sir"?'

And they would say other horrible names.

She would say, 'Yes, I can say "yes, sir."'

'So, well, say it.'

She said, 'I don't know you well enough.'

They beat her, I don't know how long. And after a while she began to
pray, and asked God to have mercy on those people.

And it wasn't too long before three white men came to my cell. One of
these men was a State Highway Patrolman and he asked me where I was
from. And I told him Ruleville. He said, 'We are going to check this.' And
they left my cell and it wasn't too long before they came back. He said, 'You
are from Ruleville all right,' and he used a curse word. And he said, 'We're
going to make you wish you was dead.'

I was carried out of that cell into another cell where they had two Negro
prisoners. The State Highway Patrolmen ordered the first Negro to take the
blackjack. The first Negro prisoner ordered me, by orders from the State
Highway Patrolman, for me to lay down on a bunk bed on my face. And
I laid on my face, the first Negro began to beat me.

And I was beat by the first Negro until he was exhausted. I was holding
my hands behind me at that time on my left side, because I suffered from
polio when I was six years old.

After the first Negro had beat until he was exhausted, the State Highway
Patrolman ordered the second Negro to take the blackjack.

The second Negro began to beat and I began to work my feet, and the State Highway Patrolman ordered the first Negro who had beat to sit on my feet – to keep me from working my feet. I began to scream and one white man got up and began to beat me in my head and tell me to hush.

One white man – my dress had worked up high – he walked over and pulled my dress – I pulled my dress down and he pulled my dress back up.

I was in jail when Medgar Evers was murdered.

All of this is on account of we want to register, to become first-class citizens. And if the Freedom Democratic Party is not seated now, I question America. Is this America, the land of the free and the home of the brave, where we have to sleep with our telephones off of the hooks because our lives be threatened daily, because we want to live as decent human beings, in America?

Thank you.

Source: http://www.americanrhetoric.com/speeches/fannielouhamercredentialscommittee.htm

Document 15   ANONYMOUS LETTER [SENT BY WHITE FBI INTELLEGENCE OFFICER WILLIAM SULLIVAN] TO MARTIN LUTHER KING, JR., NOVEMBER 1964

Although the federal bureaucracy could sometimes be an ally to the movement, it could also be an enemy. The FBI's counter-intelligence program, COINTELPRO, targeted King and other movement leaders and organizations in an attempt to undermine the civil rights movement, as this letter vividly illustrates.

King, look into your heart. You know you are a complete fraud and a great liability to all of us Negroes. White people in this country have enough frauds of their own but I am sure they don't have one at this time anywhere near your equal. You are no clergyman and you know it. I repeat you are a colossal fraud and an evil, vicious one at that . . .

King, like all frauds your end is approaching. You could have been our greatest leader . . . But you are done. Your 'honorary' degrees, your Nobel Prize (what a grim farce) and other awards will not save you. King, I repeat you are done . . .

The American public, the church organizations that have been helping – Protestant, Catholic and Jews will know you for what you are – an evil, abnormal beast. So will others who have backed you. You are done.

King, there is only one thing left for you to do. You know what it is. You have just 34 days in which to do it (this exact number has been selected for a specific reason, it has definite practical significant [sic]. You are done. There is but one way out for you. You better take it before your filthy, abnormal fraudulent self is bared to the nation.

Source: David J. Garrow, *The FBI and Martin Luther King, Jr.* (New York, 1981), pp. 125–6.

VOTING RIGHTS ACT OF 1965   **Document 16**

Ninety-five years after the adoption of the Fifteenth Amendment, US Congress finally passed legislation to enforce it.

AN ACT To enforce the fifteenth amendment to the Constitution of the United States, and for other purposes.

Be it enacted by the Senate and House of Representatives of the United States of America in Congress assembled, That this Act shall be known as the 'Voting Rights Act of 1965.'

SEC. 2. No voting qualification or prerequisite to voting, or standard, practice, or procedure shall be imposed or applied by any State or political subdivision to deny or abridge the right of any citizen of the United States to vote on account of race or color.

SEC. 3. (a) Whenever the Attorney General institutes a proceeding under any statute to enforce the guarantees of the fifteenth amendment in any State or political subdivision the court shall authorize the appointment of Federal examiners by the United States Civil Service Commission in accordance with section 6 to serve for such period of time and for such political subdivisions as the court shall determine is appropriate to enforce the guarantees of the fifteenth amendment . . .

SEC. 4. (a) To assure that the right of citizens of the United States to vote is not denied or abridged on account of race or color, no citizen shall be denied the right to vote in any Federal, State, or local election because of his failure to comply with any test or device in any State . . .

Source: http://www.ourdocuments.gov/print_friendly.php?page=transcript&doc=10 0&title=Transcript+of+Voting+Rights+Act+%281965%29

Document 17 DEMANDS PLACED ON THE DOOR OF THE CHICAGO CITY HALL BY MARTIN LUTHER KING, JR., 10 JULY 1966

King's dramatic posting of the Chicago Movement's demands on the door of City Hall consciously echoed the act of his namesake Martin Luther's posting of his Ninety-Five Theses on the Castle Church in Wittenburg, Germany, in 1517, which sparked the Protestant Reformation. King's Chicago demands reflect an expanding set of movement concerns after 1965.

Source: www.prrac.org/projects/Chicago96/king.pdf

Document 18 STOKELY CARMICHAEL, 'WHAT WE WANT', *NEW YORK REVIEW OF BOOKS*, 22 SEPTEMBER 1966

Stokely Carmichael's outline of Black Power's demands echoes much of Malcolm X's rhetoric, a year after the Black Muslim leader was assassinated, and it reflects his influence on SNCC activists at the time.

One of the tragedies of the struggle against racism is that up to now there has been no national organization which could speak to the growing militancy of young black people in the urban ghetto. There has been only a civil rights movement, whose tone of voice was adapted to an audience of liberal whites. It served as a sort of buffer zone between them and angry young blacks. None of its so-called leaders could go into a rioting community and be listened to. In a sense, I blame ourselves – together with the mass media – for what has happened in Watts, Harlem, Chicago, Cleveland, Omaha. Each time the people in those cities saw Martin Luther King get slapped, they became angry; when they saw four little black girls bombed to death, they were angrier; and when nothing happened, they were steaming. We had nothing to offer that they could see, except to go out and be beaten again. We helped to build their frustration.

For too many years, black Americans marched and had their heads broken and got shot. They were saying to the country, 'Look, you guys are supposed to be nice guys and we are only going to do what we are supposed to do – why do you beat us up, why don't you give us what we ask, why don't you straighten yourselves out?' After years of this, we are at almost the same point – because we demonstrated from a position of weakness. We cannot be expected any longer to march and have our heads broken in order to say to whites: come on, you're nice guys. For you are not nice guys. We have found you out.

An organization which claims to speak for the needs of a community – as does the Student Nonviolent Coordinating Committee – must speak in the tone of that community, not as somebody else's buffer zone. This is the significance of black power as a slogan. For once, black people are going to use the words they want to use – not just the words whites want to hear. And they will do this no matter how often the press tries to stop the use of the slogan by equating it with racism or separatism.

An organization which claims to be working for the needs of a community – as SNCC does – must work to provide that community with a position of strength from which to make its voice heard. This is the significance of black power beyond the slogan.

Black power can be clearly defined for those who do not attach the fears of white America to their questions about it. We should begin with the basic fact that black Americans have two problems: they are poor and they are black. All other problems arise from this two-sided reality: lack of education, the so-called apathy of black men. Any program to end racism must address itself to that double reality.

Almost from its beginning, SNCC sought to address itself to both conditions with a program aimed at winning political power for impoverished Southern blacks. We had to begin with politics because black Americans are a propertyless people in a country where property is valued above all. We had to work for power, because this country does not function by morality, love, and nonviolence, but by power. Thus we determined to win political power, with the idea of moving on from there into activity that would have economic effects. With power, the masses could *make or participate in making* the decisions which govern their destinies, and thus create basic change in their day-to-day lives . . .

Ultimately, the economic foundations of this country must be shaken if black people are to control their lives. The colonies of the United States – and this includes the black ghettoes within its borders, North and South – must be liberated. For a century, this nation has been like an octopus of exploitation, its tentacles stretching from Mississippi and Harlem to South America, the Middle East, southern Africa, and Vietnam; the form of exploitation varies from area to area but the essential result has been the same – a powerful few have been maintained and enriched at the expense of the poor and voiceless colored masses. This pattern must be broken. As its grip loosens here and there around the world, the hopes of black Americans become more realistic. For racism to die, a totally different America must be born . . .

The need for psychological equality is the reason why SNCC today believes that blacks must organize in the black community. Only black people can convey the revolutionary idea that black people are able to do things themselves. Only they can help create in the community an aroused and continuing black consciousness that will provide the basis for political strength. In the past, white allies have furthered white supremacy without the whites involved realizing it – or wanting it, I think. Black people must do things for themselves; they must get poverty money they will control and spend themselves; they must conduct tutorial programs themselves so that black children can identify with black people. This is one reason Africa has such importance: The reality of black men ruling their own natives gives blacks elsewhere a sense of possibility, of power, which they do not now have.

This does not mean we don't welcome help or friends. But we want the right to decide whether anyone is, in fact, our friend. In the past, black Americans have been almost the only people whom everybody and his momma could jump up and call their friends. We have been tokens, symbols, objects – as I was in high school to many young whites, who liked having 'a Negro friend.' We want to decide who is our friend, and we will not accept someone who comes to us and says: 'If you do X, Y, and Z, then I'll help you.' We will not be told whom we should choose as allies. We will not be isolated from any group or nation except by our own choice. We cannot have the oppressors telling the oppressed how to rid themselves of the oppressor.

Source: *New York Review of Books*, 22 September 1966.

Document 19   MARTIN LUTHER KING, JR., 'BEYOND VIETNAM – A TIME TO BREAK SILENCE', 4 APRIL 1967

King's 4 April 1967 speech at New York's Riverside Church was delivered exactly a year before his assassination. It marked a decisive break with the Johnson administration and alienated many movement leaders and former supporters of King.

Source: http://www.americanrhetoric.com/speeches/mlkatimetobreaksilence.htm

Document 20   REPORT OF THE NATIONAL ADVISORY COMMISSION ON CIVIL DISORDERS [KERNER COMMISSION], 29 FEBRUARY 1968

The Report of the National Advisory Commission on Civil Disorders, chaired by Illinois governor Otto Kerner, famously concluded that, 'Our nation is moving toward two societies, one black, one white – separate and unequal.'

The summer of 1967 again brought racial disorders to American cities, and with them shock, fear and bewilderment to the nation.

The worst came during a two-week period in July, first in Newark and then in Detroit. Each set off a chain reaction in neighboring communities.

On July 28, 1967, the President of the United States established this Commission and directed us to answer three basic questions:

What happened? Why did it happen? What can be done to prevent it from happening again?

To respond to these questions, we have undertaken a broad range of studies and investigations. We have visited the riot cities; we have heard many witnesses; we have sought the counsel of experts across the country.

This is our basic conclusion: Our nation is moving toward two societies, one black, one white – separate and unequal.

Reaction to last summer's disorders has quickened the movement and deepened the division. Discrimination and segregation have long permeated much of American life; they now threaten the future of every American.

This deepening racial division is not inevitable. The movement apart can be reversed. Choice is still possible. Our principal task is to define that choice and to press for a national resolution.

To pursue our present course will involve the continuing polarization of the American community and, ultimately, the destruction of basic democratic values.

The alternative is not blind repression or capitulation to lawlessness. It is the realization of common opportunities for all within a single society.

This alternative will require a commitment to national action – compassionate, massive and sustained, backed by the resources of the most powerful and the richest nation on this earth. From every American it will require new attitudes, new understanding, and, above all, new will.

The vital needs of the nation must be met; hard choices must be made, and, if necessary, new taxes enacted.

Violence cannot build a better society. Disruption and disorder nourish repression, not justice. They strike at the freedom of every citizen. The community cannot – it will not – tolerate coercion and mob rule.

Violence and destruction must be ended – in the streets of the ghetto and in the lives of people.

Segregation and poverty have created in the racial ghetto a destructive environment totally unknown to most white Americans.

What white Americans have never fully understood – but what the Negro can never forget – is that white society is deeply implicated in the ghetto. White institutions created it, white institutions maintain it and white society condones it.

It is time now to turn with all the purpose at our command to the major unfinished business of this nation. It is time to adopt strategies for action that will produce quick and visible progress. It is time to make good the promises of American democracy to all citizens – urban and rural, white and black, Spanish-surname, American Indian, and every minority group.

Our recommendations embrace three basic principles:

To mount programs on a scale equal to the dimension of the problems;

To aim these programs for high impact in the immediate future in order to close the gap between promise and performance;

To undertake new initiatives and experiments that can change the system of failure and frustration that now dominates the ghetto and weakens our society.

These programs will require unprecedented levels of funding and performance, but they neither probe deeper nor demand more than the problems which called them forth. There can be no higher priority for national action and no higher claim on the nation's conscience. . . .

Source: http://historymatters.gmu.edu/d/6545/

Document 21   MARTIN LUTHER KING, JR., 'I'VE BEEN TO THE MOUNTAINTOP', 3 APRIL 1968

King's last ever speech, delivered the evening before he was assassinated, reflects on his movement journey to Memphis and looks forward anxiously to the 'difficult days ahead'.

Source: http://mlk-kpp01.stanford.edu/index.php/encyclopedia/documentsentry/ive_been_to_the_mountaintop/

Index